The Practice of Persuasion

Also by Keith Moxey

Pieter Aertsen, Joachim Beuckelaer, and the Rise of Secular Painting in the Context of the Reformation (1977)

Peasants, Warriors, and Wives: Popular Imagery in the Reformation (1989)

Visual Theory: Painting and Interpretation, coeditor (1991)

Visual Culture: Images and Interpretation, coeditor (1994)

The Practice of Theory: Poststructuralism, Cultural Politics, and Art History (1994)

The Subjects of Art History: Historical Objects in Contemporary Perspective, coeditor (1998)

The Practice of Persuasion

Paradox and Power in Art History

Keith Moxey

Cornell University Press
ITHACA AND LONDON

First published 2001 by Cornell University Press
First printing, Cornell Paperbacks, 2001

Printed in the United States of America

Library of Congress Cataloging-in-Publication Data

Moxey, Keith P. F., 1943–
The practice of persuasion : paradox and power in art history / Keith Moxey.
p. cm.
Includes bibliographical references (p.) and index.
ISBN 0-8014-3801-2 (cloth : acid-free paper) — ISBN 0-8014-8675-0 (pbk. : acid-free paper)
1. Art—Historiography. 2. Art criticism—Methodology. I. Title.
N380 .M679 2000
700'.7'22—dc21
00-009873

Cornell University Press strives to use environmentally responsible suppliers and materials to the fullest extent possible in the publishing of its books. Such materials include vegetable-based, low-VOC inks and acid-free papers that are recycled, totally chlorine-free, or partly composed of nonwood fibers. Books that bear the logo of the FSC (Forest Stewardship Council) use paper taken from forests that have been inspected and certified as meeting the highest standards for environmental and social responsibility. For further information, visit our website at www.cornellpress.cornell.edu.

Cloth printing 10 9 8 7 6 5 4 3 2 1
Paperback printing 10 9 8 7 6 5 4 3 2 1

to Michael

Probably the tension between the need to explain an awareness of the unexplainable, between the effort to translate the signs of past reality into present discourse and the effort to save them from translation—is what characterizes and distinguishes the historian as historian. The impossible task is to lead Eurydice back from the Underworld without succumbing to the fate of Orpheus.

—Lionel Gossman, "Death in Trieste"

Contents

Illustrations

Acknowledgments

Some of the chapters in this book are based on essays which have already appeared in print, but they have all been reworked and revised for inclusion here. "Perspective, Panofsky, and the Philosophy of History" began as a lecture delivered in 1994 at the College Art Association meetings in New York, as well as at the Center for Historical and Cultural Change at the University of Virginia in the same year. I thank Ralph Cohen for this opportunity. The essay itself appeared in *New Literary History* 26 (1995), 175–86. "Motivating History" was given as a plenary lecture at the 28th Annual Conference of the Center for Medieval and Renaissance Studies at the State University of New York at Binghamton in 1994, and at the Art History Departments of Bryn Mawr and Dartmouth Colleges. I am grateful to Albert Tricomi, Steven Levine, and Ada Cohen for these invitations. That essay appeared in *Art Bulletin* 77 (1995): 392–401. Another version may be found in *Contextualizing the Renaissance: Returns to History*, ed. Albert Tricomi (New York: Brepols, 1999), 119–40. "Art History's Hegelian Unconscious" was given as a talk in the German Studies Department of Columbia University in 1996 (thanks to Michael Levine) and at the Society for the Humanities of Cornell University (thanks to Dominick LaCapra) in the same year. Other versions were given in the Art History Department of the University of Helsinki (thanks to Renja Suominen-Kokkonen and Riita Nikkula) and in the Department of Art History and Theory of the University of Otago, Dunedin (thanks to Peter Stupples) in 1997. The essay appeared in *The Subjects of Art History: Historical Objects in Contemporary Perspective*, ed. Mark Cheetham, Michael Ann Holly, and Keith Moxey (New York: Cambridge University Press, 1998),

25–51. Chapter 6 was given as "Art History after the 'Death of the Death of the Author' " at the 1997 "Recycling Culture" conference, Society for the Humanities, Cornell University (thanks to Mieke Bal); the Power Institute of Art, University of Sydney (thanks to Terry Smith); the Department of Art History and Theory of the University of Otago, Dunedin (thanks again to Peter Stupples); the State University of New York at Stony Brook (thanks to the graduate students in art history); and the Getty Institute for Visual and Cultural Studies, University of Rochester in 1998. It appeared in *Uméni/Art* 46 (1998): 174–80, and was translated into Danish in *Periskop* 7 (1999): 115–29. "Nostalgia for the Real" was delivered in 1999 at the Department of Art and Art History of the University of Stockholm (thanks to Margaretha Rossholm-Lagerlöf), the "History and Images" conference organized by the Department of History, University of Copenhagen (thanks to Axel Bolvig), and the Getty Institute for Art History and Visual Studies, University of Rochester. "History, Fiction, Memory" was a contribution to the symposium "Tilman Riemenschneider: A Late Medieval Master Sculptor" held at the National Gallery of Art in 1999. I am grateful to Julien Chapuis for the invitation to take part. It was also given at the "Historiography of Art History" conference held in 1999 at the University of Oslo (thanks to Jon-Ove Steihaug).

I want to acknowledge the graduate students who have taken courses in which some of the ideas that inform this book were worked out. Particularly helpful to this project were Christian Rattemeyer and Juan Ledezma. It was Chris Mills who drew attention to my obsession with paradox. I am also most grateful to those who read and commented upon this book in various drafts. These friends include Mieke Bal, Mark Cheetham, Janet Wolff, Eduardo Neiva, Peter Parshall, and Cathy Sousloff. Maureen Gaelens helped this technologically challenged author make the transition from manuscript to mechanically reproducible text. Jonathan Neil was responsible for final adjustments and corrections. Many thanks to both. Finally, this book is dedicated to Michael Ann Holly, the dearest and sweetest editor of them all.

KEITH MOXEY

New York City

The Practice of Persuasion

Introduction

The Politics of Persuasion

> The "dialogue" between past and present can be profitably seen in terms of its disfiguring work: history writing is clearly disfigurative in the primary sense, since it cannot leave the historical record in the same condition in which it finds it, but it should also be disfigurative in the secondary sense if it is to take account of its own enabling tropes, make itself aware of its projective or constructive figural system, and, as the final turn recognize its own disfigurement in the work of disfiguration.
>
> —Peter de Bolla, "Disfiguring History"

The following chapters are first and foremost meditations on the discipline of art history in the context of contemporary theory. They address the status of the canon, the nature of aesthetic value, the character of historical knowledge, the relation of that knowledge to fiction and memory, and the discipline's unconscious indebtedness to a particular philosophy of history. Only when considered together do these chapters betray (rather than display) a common interest or a fascination with the paradoxical power of narrative. Each, in one way or another, claims to demonstrate how the meanings with which language is invested are inevitably unstable and unfixed. Yet meaning is as inescapable as it is necessary. The very inadequacy of language as a system of signification enables us to understand its rhetorical strength, its power of persuasion. With that recognition in mind, I have two principal objectives: to encourage greater acceptance of new kinds of interpretation produced from subject positions that have so far only rarely been acknowledged in art history's institutional practice and to foster greater experimentation in defining the parameters of its disciplinary business.

As many thinkers in the late twentieth century have argued, history writing thrives on ambivalence. The trope of paradox has been crucial to analyses of language that seek to understand the promise of narrative as well as its incapacity to deliver meaning. Paradox offers us a way of conceiving of the simultaneous presence and absence of significance, the way in which sense is always haunted by its opposite. The power of paradox lies in its ability to cut both ways, a trait that admits the grip of the status quo and the enduring dictates of tradition while undermining them. Although paradox calls into question the processes of signification, it simultaneously insists that the impulse to understand the past and our relation to it demands that some sort of meaning be made. All narratives, of course, tell a tale and construct a truth. Paradox, however, reminds us that the story is only one of the many that could be derived from the same circumstances. Unlike Hegelian logic, according to which antithesis follows thesis in the creation of a synthesis that somehow reconciles the conflicting principles of the past two stages, my use of paradox implies neither movement nor reconciliation. Rather than determine a single course of action, paradox yields a multiplicity of meanings that certify a lack of closure.

If paradox is a trope, persuasion is its rhetoric. Persuasion is the result of a personal and political response to the cultural and interpretive predicament of paradox. Both in belief and conviction, persuasion attempts to create a referent that is absent by insisting that signification matters, despite the all-too-evident limitations of the sign. Emphasizing persuasion is a way of suggesting the inevitability, as well as the necessity, of motivated history writing. Language's capacity to register the particularity of different contexts and discrete subjectivities ensures the power of persuasion. The persuasive impulse emerges when the will to make meaning glances off the impossibility of its own ambition.

Pairing persuasion with paradox has radical implications for our conception of art historical scholarship. The recognition that historical interpretation must always bear the mark of the circumstances of its creation permits us to conceive of knowledge as something other than universal and absolute. In the context of contemporary theorizations of epistemology, knowledge has come to be regarded less as transhistorical than as something specific, a body of concepts suited to a particular time and place.

An appreciation of the situated quality of knowledge should not, however, result in an unthinking acceptance of relativism. Recognizing that our own perspective has no more grounding in the "real," no more forceful or compelling claims to universality than any other, does not mean that our commitment to our view is any less passionate or determined. The fact that a limited conception of knowledge must, by definition, tolerate a plethora of different and competing voices places an exceptional importance on the rhetoric of persuasion. Perceiving knowledge as something local rather than global should empower us to act more effectively and responsibly in changing cultural circumstances than pledging allegiance to the "grand narratives"—the philosophical and political systems that have hitherto dominated our view of history.

It should come as no surprise that some of the most influential concepts in contemporary theory, such as Judith Butler's "performativity," Gayatri Spivak's "strategic essentialism," Ernesto Laclau's and Chantal Mouffe's "radical democracy," or Homi Bhabha's "hybridity" are all both paradoxical and persuasive in nature.[1] As a theory of subjectivity, Butler's "performativity" at once asserts the subject's embeddedness in tradition, its formation by means of pre-scripted roles, *and* insists on its capacity to manipulate and vary those roles for its own purposes. Spivak's "strategic essentialism" suggests that there is nothing fixed about gendered identity *and* allows for the political potential inherent in claims to essentialism. The "radical democracy" of Laclau and Mouffe holds out the possibility of a government responsive to all interests *and* recognizes that cultures are deeply divided by irresolvable differences. And Homi Bhabha's "hybridity" implies that a subaltern people can both acquire the manners and customs of its oppressors *and* use them to question the very identity of those who are imitated.

Paradoxes proliferate in my study as well. Chapter 1 considers the fate of art history writing after historicism. It challenges the traditional structures of a teleological philosophy of history, argu-

1. See Judith Butler, *Gender Trouble: Feminism and the Subversion of Identity* (New York: Routledge, 1990); Gayatri Spivak, "Subaltern Studies: Deconstructing Historiography," in *In Other Worlds: Essays in Cultural Politics* (New York: Routledge, 1988), 197–221; Ernesto Laclau and Chantal Mouffe, *Hegemony and Socialist Strategy: Towards a Radical Democratic Politics* (London: Verso, 1985); and Homi Bhabha, "Of Mimicry and Man: The Ambivalence of Colonial Discourse," in *The Location of Culture* (London: Routledge, 1994), 85–92.

ing that it has been responsible for dangerously nationalist forms of historical interpretation, and acknowledges that philosophical agendas are a prerequisite for the production of historical narratives. While rejecting the naturalized Hegelian concepts that have so deeply marked the history of art, it calls for a motivated history, a narrative marked by political principles engaged with the cultural concerns of the present day.

The next chapter examines the relation between history writing, fiction, and memory. An analysis of the historiography on the late medieval German sculptor Tilman Riemenschneider suggests that art history's attempt, after the Second World War, to distance itself from the interpretive excesses of German art writing during the Nazi era has often led to a reductive positivism, a form of history reluctant to engage in "strong" interpretation and thus impoverished of its narrative potential. The paradox of this essay lies in the fact that it both criticizes the interpretations put forward by the nationalists and argues that art historians should demonstrate a greater willingness to forsake the alleged neutrality of the "facts" for forms of understanding that attempt to make the past relevant and significant for the present and future. Rather than suggest that past historians somehow failed to make historically justifiable arguments, I claim that their interpretations cannot convince us today because we find their assumptions and their conclusions repugnant. Their work therefore is to be rejected as unpersuasive rather than untruthful, for rhetoric can only be countered by another, contrary, form of argumentation.

The third chapter discusses the role of the canon in art historical discourse. I argue that although the canon's self-evident status needs constant questioning, it is difficult to conceive of an art historical discipline without a set (or sets) of works around which its activities might focus. This draws attention to disciplinary conflicts: tradition is not value-free, and there is no reason to believe that what has been privileged in the past should continue to be exalted in the present, yet art history cannot proceed without principles on which those works most relevant to its deliberations can be selected.

Chapter 4 reflects on the metaphor of Renaissance perspective in the historical writing of Erwin Panofsky. His famous essay "Perspective as Symbolic Form" has radical and conservative moments.

The author claims both that pictorial perspective is a device that varies according to culture and history and that the Italian Renaissance's version of this spatial construct coincides most fully with modern theories of vision. My essay is critical of the latter claim, as well as of its use as a metaphor for the stability and certainty of historical knowledge. Just as the Renaissance artist could depict an illusionistic space in a way that corresponds to our own perception, the argument goes, so humanist scholars (and, by extension, Panofsky himself) were able to distinguish past from present in a way that guaranteed the distance necessary to obtain an objective view of history. I counter that the historian cannot escape Nietzschean "perspectivism." Meaning can be found in the past only through the imposition of subjective grids or structures of understanding that can never coincide with the historical events themselves. There are, in other words, no "symbolic forms" that might secure the passage from representation to reality. My argument both criticizes linear perspective's potential as a metaphor of knowledge and holds that a perspective (i.e., a point of view) is nevertheless an indispensable weapon in the historian's heuristic arsenal.

The fifth chapter both affirms and denies art history's need for an aesthetic frame. I argue that the discipline can open its borders to a variety of forms of visual culture while acknowledging that this gesture can be accomplished productively only if art history fields persuasive claims to sustain the idea of art as a distinct form of cultural discourse.

In the concluding chapter, paradox surrounds the authorial voice, arguing that it both does and does not matter "who is speaking." On the one hand, authorial identity cannot matter because there can never be a one-to-one correspondence between a text and its author. The text necessarily obeys conventions that antedate the intervention of any particular subjectivity, so that there is no transparent passage between them. On the other hand, an author's identity matters in that his or her cultural specificity can be persuasively asserted so as to break the universalist claims to knowledge associated with the "voice from nowhere."

Needless to say, these paradoxes swim against the current of much contemporary cultural commentary. My concern with the theoretical and philosophical assumptions underlying art historical practice resists the current backlash against the so-called theoretical excesses of the 1980s and 1990s. There appears to be an undisguised desire for normalcy, for a return to a conception of history as a communal craft, one that depends on shared assumptions and common values and forgets the strident conflicts of the "culture wars." Deliberately misunderstanding the "strategic essentialism" that characterized these social and political struggles, those who desire to return to "business as usual" attempt to dismiss them by wielding theoretical weapons forged by their opponents. Arguing that the claims of identity politics are as essentializing as those of the status quo, neoconservative critics seek to tar the innovators with the same brush that was once brandished against them. In doing so, they fail to appreciate that the import of the new claims is political and strategic, rather than epistemological and universal. Persuasion is discounted or refused because of its dependence on paradox.

Indeed, it sometimes seems as if art history were experiencing a return to order. More often than not, this compulsion takes the form of a return to "the primacy of the object." The work of art supposedly speaks for itself and is best elucidated by means of the stratagems developed in the history of the history of art, rather than through references to critical theories imported from elsewhere in the humanities.[2] *The Practice of Persuasion* takes a stand against this trend. It not only questions the "autonomy" of art by suggesting that it is a form of cultural discourse comparable to any other, but as a consequence it also implies that there are no grounds—especially aesthetic ones—upon which art history can privilege its protocols above those of any other humanistic discipline. Dedicated to the proposition that there is nothing fixed about art history's boundaries, this book argues that it is only when the discipline's traditional assumptions have been questioned and revised that its historical accounts demonstrate a compelling narrative interest for the age in which we live.

The politics of persuasion might thus be articulated as an attempt to insist, in the context of symbolic determination and in the midst of established historiographic traditions, that we have the ca-

2. See, for example, Thomas Crow, *The Intelligence of Art* (Chapel Hill: University of North Carolina Press, 1999).

pacity to manipulate the codes and conventions of our culture in such a way as to alter the "morals" which animate our accounts of the past. The politics of persuasion eludes any one agenda: its ambition is to lay the theoretical foundations upon which different forms of knowledge, responding to subject positions previously suppressed or elided, may at last find their voices. If there is nothing necessary about the current shape of our knowledge, then the future will be determined on the basis of argument. In the absence of a consensus about meaning, truth-claims can be established, challenged, and debated only by persuasion.

CHAPTER ONE

Art History's Hegelian Unconscious

Naturalism as Nationalism in the Study of Early Netherlandish Painting

> Historicism contents itself with establishing a causal connection between various moments in history. But no fact that is a cause is for that reason historical. It became historical posthumously, as it were, through events that may be separated from it by thousands of years. A historian who takes this as his point of departure stops telling the sequence of events like the beads of a rosary. Instead, he grasps the constellation which his own era has formed with a definite earlier one. Thus he establishes a conception of the present as the "time of the now" which is shot through with chips of Messianic time.
>
> —Walter Benjamin, "Theses on the Philosophy of History"

> The history of art, through its continuous mediation of past and present art, can become a paradigm for a history that is to show the "development of this present." . . . But art history can take on this function only if it itself overcomes the organon-type principle of the history of style, and thus liberates itself from traditionalism and its metaphysics of supratemporal beauty.
>
> —Hans Robert Jauss, "History of Art and Pragmatic History"

In the context of notions of history marked by what has come to be known as the "linguistic turn," the historiography of the history of art can be read with different eyes.[1] Once we abandon the

1. The conception of language as something opaque rather than transparent was first brought home to historians by Michel Foucault. Foucault used the term *discursive practices* to cover all aspects of the production of cultural meaning, thus claiming the capacity to read social formations as texts. Some of his most influential historical readings are *The Order of Things*, trans. Alan Sheridan (London: Tavistock, 1970); *Madness and Civilization*, trans. Richard Howard (London: Tavistock, 1971); *The Archaeology of Knowledge*, trans. Alan Sheridan (London: Tavistock, 1972); and *Discipline and Punish*, trans. Alan Sheridan (London: Allen Lane, 1979). In the English-speaking world, it was Hayden White who, in a series of powerfully argued books and essays, insisted on a textual understanding of the past and a rhetorical conception of the text. See his *Metahistory: The Historical Imagination in*

idea that written histories correspond with events that may have taken place in the past—so that the concept of truth as something found rather than constructed is irrelevant to the historian's project—the status of history as text acquires new significance. Just as poststructuralism has altered our views about history, so it has transformed our attitudes toward historiography. Instead of being viewed as the record of previous attempts to do justice to the past, attempts that need to be corrected and superseded as subsequent generations of historians discover new and more pertinent "facts" among the "documents" or "archives" relating to the period under scrutiny, the textual history of the discipline can now be examined from a different perspective. If the importance of the subject position of the author is taken into consideration, if the writer's location in the present is acknowledged as an integral part of his or her account of the past, then it becomes possible to analyze the written record of the history of art with an eye to the cultural values and ideological commitments with which the authors invested their texts, and to determine the social function of those texts at the time of their composi-

---

Nineteenth-Century Europe (Baltimore: Johns Hopkins University Press, 1973); *Tropics of Discourse: Essays in Cultural Criticism* (Baltimore: Johns Hopkins University Press, 1978); and *The Content of the Form: Narrative Discourse and Historical Representation* (Baltimore: Johns Hopkins University Press, 1987). Much the same approach has been applied to intellectual history by Dominick LaCapra, *Rethinking Intellectual History: Texts, Contexts, Language* (Ithaca: Cornell University Press, 1983); *History and Criticism* (Ithaca: Cornell University Press, 1985); *Soundings in Critical Theory* (Ithaca: Cornell University Press, 1989). The implications of the concept of history as text also have been explored by Robert Berkhofer Jr., *Beyond the Great Story: History as Text and Discourse* (Cambridge: Harvard University Press, 1995), and Philippe Carrard, *Poetics of the New History: French Historical Discourse from Braudel to Chartier* (Baltimore: Johns Hopkins University Press, 1992). The "linguistic turn" has had important implications for our understanding of historical knowledge, particularly the notion of historical objectivity. See Peter Novick, *That Noble Dream: The "Objectivity Question" and the American Historical Profession* (New York: Cambridge University Press, 1988), and Robert D'Amico, *Historicism and Knowledge* (London: Routledge, 1989). The influence of Foucault can be discerned in the movement known as the "new historicism." In the work of Stephen Greenblatt, Louis Montrose, and others, a recognition of the textuality of history, of the opacity of the past, has resulted in the production of texts that often call attention to authors' involvement with contemporary cultural issues as part of their accounts of the past. See Stephen Greenblatt, *Renaissance Self-Fashioning: From More to Shakespeare* (Chicago: University of Chicago Press, 1980); *Shakespearean Negotiations: The Circulation of Social Energy in Renaissance England* (Oxford: Clarendon Press, 1988); and *Marvelous Possessions: The Wonder of the New World* (Chicago: University of Chicago Press, 1991). For an account of the British counterpart of this movement, known as "cultural materialism," see Scott Wilson, *Cultural Materialism: Theory and Practice* (Oxford: Blackwell, 1995).

tion. Such an approach to historiography serves to enrich its traditional status as part of the cultural history of ideas by associating it with the notion of ideological criticism or discourse analysis.

With the new centrality ascribed to the text of history in mind, I have become intrigued by the notion of teleological direction that informs so much of the historiography on early Netherlandish painting. The insistence with which scholars in this field invoke the notion of progress has prompted me to ask two related questions. First, what is the ideological function of the concept of a teleologically-directed concept of history—why have so many scholars subscribed to the idea of historical development or progress? And second, what happens to the concept of history once the idea of development, the teleological imperative, is forsaken? If, as Jean-François Lyotard suggests, the age of "grand narratives" is over, then what might be a philosophy of history appropriate to our poststructural or postmodern condition?[2]

Teleological accounts of early Netherlandish painting obviously owe their greatest debt to the philosophy of Hegel. Art history, like history itself, has tended to assume that the events of the past make sense: there is an immanent logic in the succession of artistic styles, which it is the task of the historian to describe. In calling this assumption "Hegelian," I am clearly using the term in its broadest sense. If the historiography of art history is Hegelian, it is because the fundamental strategies of its approach to history—the idea of purposive or teleological development, the belief that the sequence of styles characterizing different periods embodies an inherent principle of historical change, and the conviction that certain artists transcend their historical circumstances in order to enable great artistic transformations—all figure prominently in its historical narratives.[3] While such strategies are so unquestioningly invoked as to appear to be the very conditions of possibility for art

2. Jean-François Lyotard, *The Postmodern Condition: A Report on Knowledge*, trans. Geoff Bennington and Brian Massumi (Minneapolis: University of Minnesota Press, 1984).

3. Art history's dependence on Hegelian ideas has always been recognized; see, for example, Ernst Gombrich, *In Search of Cultural History* (Oxford: Clarendon Press, 1969), and his article "The Father of Art History: A Reading of the Lectures on Aesthetics of G. W. F. Hegel (1770–1831)," in *Tributes: Interpreters of Our Cultural Tradition* (Ithaca: Cornell University Press, 1984), 51–69. The Hegelian tradition has been viewed favorably by James Elkins, "Art History without Theory," *Critical Inquiry* 4 (1988): 354–78, and unfavorably by Stephen Melville, "The Temptation of New Perspectives," *October* 52 (1990): 3–15. For a discussion of the

history as a practice, I will argue that they have histories of their own. The assumption that these clichés of art historical interpretation actually match the structure of events—that such concepts reflect the "order of things"—is what this chapter seeks to contest.

As we shall see, the impulse to tell purposive narratives, a tendency promoted by Hegel's philosophy of history, effectively coincided with the nationalist politics of nineteenth- and twentieth-century Europe. Hegel's view of history must thus be considered only one aspect of a dense set of ideas that constitutes the discursive practice of art history. In referring to the discipline's "Hegelian unconscious," I intend social as well as psychoanalytic associations. The values that characterize the signifying systems of art history's professional existence may in all fairness be described as ideological. They are, in other words, ideas that betray attitudes and prejudices associated with the historical periods in which they are manifested. Art historical ideology carries the raced, classed, and gendered convictions of those responsible for its production as well as its reception. Needless to say, the full complexity of art history's unconscious freight cannot be unpacked in this study of the epistemological underpinnings of the history of northern Renaissance art. I am principally concerned here to articulate the ways in which Hegel's ideas have intersected with some of the other less explicit agendas of art history's professional discourse.

To exemplify the workings of the Hegelian unconscious within the context of northern Renaissance art, I will concentrate in this chapter on the historiography of Hans Memling.[4] I am interested

---

relevance of the Hegelian tradition for contemporary art history, see Hans Belting, *The End of Art History*, trans. Christopher Wood (Chicago: University of Chicago Press, 1987) and *Das Ende der Kunstgeschichte. Eine Revision nach Zehn Jahren* (Munich: Beck, 1995).

4. For useful introductions to the historiography of early Netherlandish painting, see Suzanne Sulzberger, *La Réhabilitation des primitifs flamands, 1802–1867* (Brussels: Palais des Académies, 1961); Francis Haskell, "Huizinga and the 'Flemish Renaissance,' " in *History and Its Images: Art and the Interpretation of the Past* (New Haven: Yale University Press, 1993), 431–95; and Bernhard Ridderbos and Henk van Veen, eds., "*Om iets te weten van de oude meesters.*" *De Vlaamse Primitieven—herontdekking, waardering en onderzoek* (Nijmegen: Uitgeverij SUN, 1995). W. E. Krul's contribution to this last book, "Realisme, Renaissance en nationalisme: cultuurhistorische opvattingen over de Oudnederlandse schilderkunst tussen 1860 en 1920," was especially useful in the preparation of this chapter. I am grateful to Maryan Ainsworth for this reference. In "Flemish versus Netherlandish: A Discourse of Naturalism," *Renaissance Quarterly* 51 (1998): 1–33, Lisa Deam draws attention to some of the nationalist disputes concerning the origins and develop-

not only in the forces that brought this painter to scholarly light, but also in those that led to the eclipse of his reputation. What sorts of narratives have been told about this artist and what are the cultural values that inform them? What follows is by no means intended to be a complete review of the Memling literature. Instead, I have selectively chosen certain authors whose texts seem emblematic of both the attitudes that supported the esteem in which he was once held and those that led to his fall from favor. In discussing Memling, it will be necessary to refer to the historiography of two other artists, Jan van Eyck and Hugo van der Goes, on which his status can be seen to depend. The second of the pair is particularly relevant to this project, for it could be said that Memling's prestige is structurally related to Hugo's—as one rises in scholarly estimation, the other falls, demonstrating a historiographic hydraulics powered by changing attitudes toward the philosophy of history.

This account of the Memling historiography must also pay attention to the operation of what Ernst Gombrich has called "Hegel's wheel."[5] Historians often suggest that different aspects of a particular culture are related to one another by historical developments

---

ment of naturalism that are addressed in this essay. She focuses particularly on the use of the word "Netherlandish" to describe painting that might more properly be called "Flemish." She points out that the term "Netherlandish" is associated with attempts to claim the fifteenth-century artistic tradition of present-day Belgium for Germany. For a review of the Memling literature, see Vida Joyce Hull, *Hans Memlinc's Paintings for the Hospital at Saint John in Bruges* (New York: Garland, 1981), chap. 7, and Lori van Biervliet, "De roem van Memling," in *Hans Memling: Essays*, ed. Dirk de Vos (Bruges: Ludion, 1994), 109–24. The following reference came to my attention after this chapter was complete: Till-Holger Borchert, "A Moving Expression of Most Sincere Devotion and Piety. Aspects of Memling's Rediscovery in Early Nineteenth-Century Germany." In *Memling Studies: Proceedings of the International Colloquium* (Bruges, 10–12 November 1994), ed. Hélène Verougstraete et al., (Louvain: Uitgererij Peters, 1997).

5. Gombrich, *In Search of Cultural History*, 10. The literature on the concept of historicism is vast. The term has been used quite variously and indeed contradictorily. Some authors have used it to insist on the importance of historical location for the interpretation of human culture, whereas others have used it to describe a teleological view of the past. See, for example, Friedrich Meinecke, *Historicism: The Rise of a New Historical Outlook*, trans. J. Anderson (New York: Herder and Herder, 1972); Maurice Mandelbaum, *The Problem of Historical Knowledge: An Answer to Relativism* (New York: Liveright Pub., [1938?]); George Iggers, *The German Conception of History: The National Tradition of Historical Thought from Herder to the Present* (Middletown, Conn.: Wesleyan University Press, 1968); D'Amico, *Historicism and Knowledge*; and Paul Hamilton, *Historicism* (London: Routledge, 1996). For attacks on the concept of historicism when understood as a teleology, see Karl Popper, *The Poverty of Historicism* (London: Routledge, 1994) and *The Open Society and Its Enemies*, 2 vols. (Princeton: Princeton University Press, 1966). The importance of the

characteristic of the culture as a whole, in the same way that the spokes of a wheel are related to its hub. According to this view, all facets of a culture—which is to say all of the spokes, such as art, literature, politics—may be "explained" by means of a broader historical movement, the hub (i.e., the "spirit of the age"), from which each individual aspect is presumed to radiate outward. I will argue that the assumption that cultural relationships are, by definition, meaningful fails to recognize the active role of the historian in the construction of historical narratives. In the light of poststructuralist theory, historians might acknowledge that the "hub" that accounts for the significance of the "spokes" is not found in the past, but placed there in the present by the pattern-making activity of the historian.

Before Memling became caught up in the wheels of a teleologically oriented historiography, he attracted the imagination of early-nineteenth-century critics. Embodying that period's incipient nationalism and conception of the artist-as-genius, the romantic movement found in the visual culture of northern Europe an artist who seemed to personify the virtues of the Germanic race but at the same time displayed an extraordinary capacity to express the piety that was part of the culture of the Middle Ages. The German literary figure Friedrich Schlegel, for example, was living in Paris when works of art confiscated by the victorious armies of Napoleon were displayed in the Louvre. Amidst this booty, the objects that excited his most profound admiration were those that exemplified the spirit of selfless devotion he identified with the medieval imagination. Departing from the prevailing preference for the Italian Renaissance, he saw exceptional qualities in the art of the Middle Ages that had been unjustly neglected. More important for my purposes, his appreciation for medieval art enabled him to sing the praises of German art. Making no distinction between the artistic production of Germany and that of the Netherlands, he articulates his reasons for revering the northern virtues of van Eyck and Memling in the following terms:

> We must not however forget that in the heyday of the older Netherlandish School both the general and the particular existed harmoniously side by side; as in the work of van Eyck and Hemmelink

---

concept in art history has been described by Catherine Soussloff, "Historicism," in *Encyclopedia of Aesthetics* (New York: Oxford University Press, 1998), 2:407–12.

[Memling], the deeply symbolic quality of devotion and sacred beauty and the emotional German strain are united. . . . In addition there is an evocation of that merry German life very clearly depicted according to the contemporary manner and custom, in the varied expressions of the other faces and secondary figures as well as in the fantastic splendor and daintiness of the colorful costumes.[6]

Memling's *Moreel Triptych* (fig. 1) is among the paintings Schlegel selects for special scrutiny. After comparing the earlier artist with Dürer, in his eyes the acme of old German painting, Schlegel commends Memling for his gentler, more peaceful spirit.

The faces are remarkably more genuinely German than is usually the case among the oldest Netherlandish painters. Here, in this admirable and relatively little known painter, one is offered a view into the as yet unknown world of old German art history. This painting could be a model for the way in which the solitary and rural circumstances of the lives of the saints should be handled. It exhales a moving expression of his deepest devotion and piety.[7]

What is remarkable about Schlegel's criticism is the way in which Christian piety and nationalism interlock so as to mutually implicate and sustain one another. The pious spirit of the Middle Ages is identified as German, and what is German is identified with the spirituality of a bygone age.

The romantic view of Memling as an exemplary Christian artist informed much of the literature throughout the nineteenth century and often granted him a higher status even than that of Jan

6. Gert Schiff, ed., "Friedrich Schlegel. From *Descriptions of Paintings from Paris and the Netherlands in the Years 1802 to 1804*. From Second Supplement of Old Paintings, Spring, 1804," trans. Peter Wortsman and Gert Schiff, in *German Essays on Art History* (New York: Continuum, 1988), 71–72.

7. Friedrich Schlegel, *Kritische Friedrich Schlegel Ausgabe*, vol. 4, *Ansichten und Ideen von der christlichen Kunst*, ed. Hans Eichner (Munich: Ferdinand Schöning, 1959), 44–45. "Die Gesichter sind auffallend mehr eigentlich deutsch, als sie sonst bei den ältesten niederländischen Malern zu sein pflegen. Hier in diesem vortrefflichen und verhältnismässig nicht so berühmten Maler öffnet sich der Blick in eine noch unbekannte Weltgegend der altdeutschen Kunstgeschichte. Dieses Gemälde könnte ein Vorbild sein, wie man landschaftliche und einsiedlerische Gegenstände der Heiligengeschichte zu behandeln hat. Es atmet durchaus in ihm ein rührende Ausdruck der innigsten Andacht und Frömmigkeit." This and all following translations are my own.

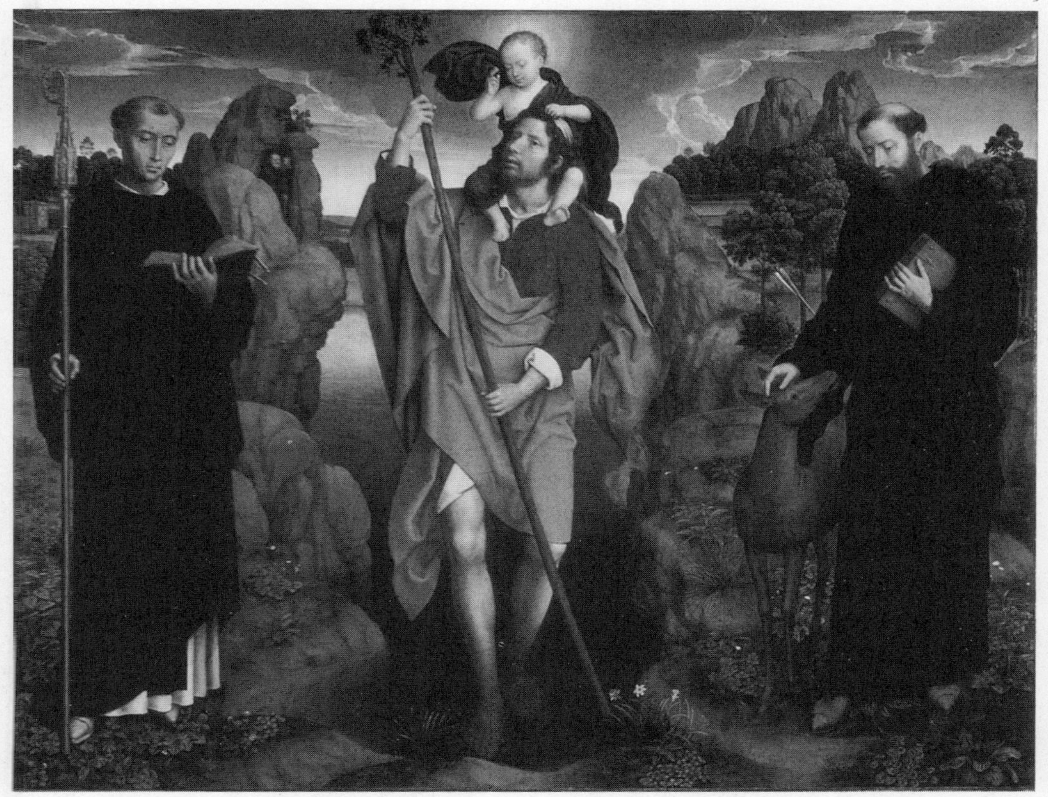

1. Hans Memling, *St. Christopher Carrying the Christ Child* (center panel of the *Moreel Triptych*), 1484. Oil on wood. Groeningenmuseum, Bruges. Courtesy of Erich Lessing/Art Resource, New York.

van Eyck, the historiographic hero of the twentieth century. A late example of this romantic tendency is found in James Weale's monograph, published in 1901, almost exactly a century after Schlegel's writings had resulted in the development of a historical interest in early Netherlandish painting. Weale, a convert to Catholicism, spent much of his life in Bruges, searching for archival evidence to document the lives of early Flemish painters. According to him, Memling was the leading Flemish artist of the fifteenth century.

> John van Eyck saw with his eyes, Memlinc with his soul. John studied, copied and reproduced with marvellous accuracy the models he had before him. Memlinc, doubtless, studied and copied, but he did

> more; he meditated and reflected; his whole soul went into his work, and he idealised and glorified, and, so to say, transfigured the models which he had before him. . . . As compared with the other masters of the Flemish school, he is the most poetical and the most musical; many of his pictures are perfect little gems.[8]

Why is there an opposition enunciated here between copying and studying the model and meditating and reflecting on it? Why is Memling's soul opposed to van Eyck's eyes? How did the imitation of nature become associated with the secular and the worldly, and idealism identified with the spiritual and the transcendent?

The answers to these questions lie in the revolutionary paradigm of historical consciousness that was developed in the first half of the nineteenth century in the philosophy of Hegel. While some aspects of his philosophy of history coincided with and further developed tendencies already present in romanticism—for example, the importance ascribed to nationalism—other features represented a radical break with the romantic sensibility. One of the most important of these differences lies in Hegel's conception of historical movement or progress. Romantic philosophers, such as J. G. Herder, had embraced a relativistic notion of history, placing an emphasis on the individuality and autonomy of cultures and nations at different moments in time.[9] Believing that the divine plan that lies behind the particularity of historical moments is inscrutable, Herder did not try to detect a pattern in the past. Hegel, on the other hand, conceived of history as a process in which it was possible to trace the workings of the "spirit" through time. In the Hegelian dialectic, history possessed an immanent logic with a teleological purpose, namely, the fulfillment of the spirit.

8. James Weale, *Hans Memlinc* (London: George Bell, 1901), 80. This passage paraphrases Eugene Fromentin's 1876 comparison of the two artists in *Les Maîtres d'autrefois*, ed. Pierre Moisy (Paris: Garnier Freres, 1972), 279. Both passages are quoted by Hull, *Hans Memlinc's Paintings*, 210–11. For Weale, see Lori van Biervliet, *Leven en Werk van W. H. James Weale. Een Engels Kunsthistoricus in Vlaanderen in de 19e Eeuw* (Brussels: Paleis der Academien, 1991).

9. Iggers, *German Conception of History*, 35. The correspondence between Romantic and poststructuralist attitudes toward history—according to which the local and specific is more important than the general and the universal, and the past is defined as something essentially inaccessible and incomprehensible—has been pointed out by Hans Kellner, "Introduction: Describing Redescriptions," in *A New Philosophy of History*, ed. Frank Ankersmit and Hans Kellner (Chicago: University of Chicago Press, 1995), 15.

The nationalism of the romantics, which had depended largely on a sense of the relative worth of different cultures and of different moments in time, was transformed in Hegel's thought by being awarded historical purpose and drive. Hegel conceived of history as a history of nations rather than of individuals or groups, for it was through nations that the spirit or *Volksgeist* of different peoples found its historical manifestation. The political appeal of such a philosophical doctrine for nineteenth-century Europe, which saw the attainment of nationhood by a whole host of countries, including major political powers on the scale of Germany and Italy, cannot be overestimated.[10] New nations could claim a role in the momentous epic of the realization of the spirit, a teleologically structured narrative that gave new significance to hindsight.

Several generations of art historians followed Hegel in seeing art as a manifestation of transcendent values. Not surprisingly, it was in those qualities of works of art with which Kant, in 1790, had most closely identified aesthetic response—namely, the formal properties of line, shape, color, and so on—that scholars believed they could discern the material embodiment and operation of the spirit.[11] These formal properties, gathered together under the rubric of style, became the focus of art historical attention.[12] The equation of style with the passage of the spirit made it possible to give color and form to the immanent forces at work in history. In an age in which knowledge was often metaphorically fig-

10. For a discussion of the creation of the nation-states of Europe in the nineteenth century, see Eric Hobsbawm and Thomas Ranger, eds., *The Invention of Tradition* (Cambridge: Cambridge University Press, 1983), and Benedict Anderson, *Imagined Communities: Reflections on the Origin and Spread of Nationalism* (New York: Verso, 1991).

11. Immanuel Kant, "The Analytic of the Beautiful," in *Critique of Aesthetic Judgement*, trans. James Meredith (Oxford: Oxford University Press, 1952), 41–89.

12. For the importance of the concept of style for art historical practice, see Meyer Schapiro, "Style," in *Anthropology Today*, ed. A. L. Kroeber (Chicago: University of Chicago Press, 1953), 287–312; Ernst Gombrich, "Norm and Form: The Stylistic Categories of Art History and Their Origins in Renaissance Ideals," in *Norm and Form: Studies in the Art of the Renaissance* (London: Phaidon, 1971), 81–98; Gombrich, "Style," in *International Encyclopedia of the Social Sciences*, ed. David Sills (New York: Macmillan, 1968–79), 15:352–61; Willibald Sauerländer, "From Stylus to Style: Reflections on the Fate of a Notion," *Art History* 6 (1983): 253–70; George Kubler, "Toward a Reductive Theory of Visual Style," in *The Concept of Style*, rev. ed., ed. Berel Lang (Ithaca: Cornell University Press, 1987), 163–73; and Svetlana Alpers, "Style Is What You Make It: The Visual Arts Once Again," in *The Concept of Style*, 137–62.

ured as vision, it is not surprising that the history of art should have sought disciplinary status as the history of the visible, as opposed to history proper, which was to remain the history of the textual.

The importance of realism as a European style in the middle of the nineteenth century affected the way in which art historians assessed the stylistic record of previous ages. If realism was to be viewed as the culmination of a transhistorical process, then the task of the Hegelian scholar was to explain how this result came about. Because of the dialectical nature of Hegel's own vision of the past, his system afforded historians a means of understanding those periods that seemed to progress toward the ideal of nineteenth-century realism as well as those that seemed to move counter to it. As Gombrich points out, even if it proved difficult to argue that the art—say, of Byzantium—might be considered a prelude to realism, its value could be located in the way it constituted a dialectical antithesis to another development—and that the combination ultimately represented an advance toward the present. From the conflation or reconciliation of the opposites contained in the thesis and the antithesis, a new synthesis emerges. Hegelianism could thus be said to have licensed the practice of an ecumenical history of art.[13]

The dialectical tension between the Renaissance and the Middle Ages in Hegel's account of the liberation of the spirit, a tension that reiterated the difference that the Renaissance itself had discerned between its own culture and that of preceding ages (a contrast most forcefully articulated for art historians in Vasari's *Lives of the Artists*), proved immensely influential in privileging realism or naturalism as the leading style of the history of art. According to Hegel, the Renaissance was a period in which human beings rejected the spiritual and psychological constraints of religion in or-

13. Gombrich, "The Father of Art History," 65: "Today it is considered scientific to eradicate the concept of decline from the art historian's vocabulary wherever possible, so as to allot every era that was once condemned, its rightful place in the chain of development. The vindication of Gothic art in the eighteenth century was accepted even by Hegel. Later, following in the tracks of Burckhardt, Wölfflin reinstated Baroque art, Wickhoff defended Roman art, Riegl the art of late antiquity, and Max Dvorák the catacomb paintings and El Greco. Walter Friedländer completely freed Mannerist art from the stigma of decline, and Millard Meiss undertook a positive evaluation of the painting of the late Trecento. At the moment we are even witnessing a revival of respect for French nineteenth-century Salon painting, which until recently was still considered to be the ultimate in kitsch."

der to immerse themselves in the secular study of the natural world.[14] Jacob Burckhardt, the first art historian to put Hegel's ideas to work in historical interpretation, used the notion of the spirit's turn toward nature as a means of understanding the realistic quality of Italian art of the fifteenth century.[15] In Burckhardt's eyes, the new naturalism, which was antithetical to the traditional content of the devotional art of the Middle Ages, was more important than the revival of antiquity with which the Renaissance had previously been identified.

> The work of art gives progressively more than the Church demands; in addition to religious matters, it now furnishes an impression of the real world; the artist dedicates himself to the research and representation of the outer appearance of things and gradually grasps the human figure as well as the spatial environment in all its manifestations.[16]

Burckhardt's interpretation of Italian Renaissance art underscores two Hegelian points. First and foremost, it establishes a form/content distinction that empowers the history of art to become a history of style. Secondly, it defines the artist's interest in the world of appearances as something which is at odds with the representation of spiritual truths.

The contrast with Schlegel's romantic criticism of early Flemish painting could not be more striking. For Schlegel, spirituality and nationalism are indistinguishable from one another. The work of art does not allow a separation of form from content, so that the history of art cannot be identified with only one aspect of the equation. Schlegel's respect for the unity of the work—its indivisibil-

14. Wallace Ferguson, *The Renaissance in Historical Thought: Five Centuries of Interpretation* (Cambridge: Riverside Press, 1948), 171–72.

15. For a discussion of the ambivalence of Burckhardt's attitude toward Hegel, see Michael Ann Holly, *Panofsky and the Foundations of Art History* (Ithaca: Cornell University Press, 1984), 30–33, and *Past Looking: Historical Imagination and the Rhetoric of the Image* (Ithaca: Cornell University Press, 1996), 29–63.

16. Jacob Burckhardt, *Der Cicerone. Eine Einleitung zum Genuss der Kunstwerke Italiens*, ed. Wilhelm Bode (Leipzig: Seemann, 1879), 524: "Das Kunstwerk gibt zunächst mehr als die Kirche verlangt; ausser den religiosen Beziehungen gewährt es jetzt ein Ausbild der wirklichen Welt; der Künstler vertieft sich in die Erforschung und Darstellung des äussern Scheines der Dinge und gewinnt der menschlichen Gestalt sowohl als räumlichen Umgebung allmählich alle ihre Erscheinungsweisen ab."

ity—also highlights its autonomy, the sense that it is not part of some larger scheme of things. The work must be appreciated for its distinctive qualities, not for those that relate it to others. In light of this contrast between Burckhardt and Schlegel, it is easier to understand Weale's reading of Memling and van Eyck. Weale was a belated romantic who preferred Memling's spiritualism to van Eyck's naturalism. Writing in the context of Hegelian art history, however, he uses the methodological tools of his opponents to defend his hero. Accepting the distinction between form and content, Weale identifies van Eyck's naturalism with the material and the secular. Because naturalism is worldly, idealism must be spiritual. Where one artist merely studied and copied nature, the other idealized and glorified it. Where van Eyck is the eye, Memling is the soul.

Weale's defense of Memling, however, could not long withstand the identification of naturalism with the secular spirit of the Renaissance. It is ironic that the eyes rather than the soul should have revealed the march of the spirit. Not only could the age of realism identify with the age of naturalism, but Burckhardt's 1860 translation of Hegel's liberation of human consciousness into the age of individualism also meant that the nineteenth century had another reason to view the Renaissance as a mirror image of itself.[17] Moreover, the consequences of the value ascribed to naturalism, for Memling's reputation, were exacerbated by the nationalism of nineteenth- and twentieth-century art historical writing. Many art historians sought to claim that naturalism, the most prestigious of the styles of the past, had its origins in their own national traditions. Even Burckhardt, who had praised the art of Renaissance Italy on the grounds of its naturalism, did so out of the sympathy he felt for Italian patriots who were calling for the unification of Italy.[18]

17. Jacob Burckhardt, *The Civilization of the Renaissance in Italy*, trans. S. G. C. Middlemore (London: Penguin Books, 1990).

18. For Burckhardt's receptiveness to the political aspirations of Italian nationalists, see Wilhelm Dilthey's review of *The Civilization* in *Selected Works*, vol. 4, ed. Rudolf Makkreel and Frithjof Rodi (Princeton: Princeton University Press, 1996), 271–77, cited by Catherine Soussloff, *The Absolute Artist: The Historiography of a Concept* (Minneapolis: University of Minnesota Press, 1997), 88. For Burckhardt's political alienation following the failed revolutions of 1848 and his disenchantment with the liberal nationalist convictions of his youth, see Michael Ann Holly, "Burckhardt and the Ideology of the Past," *History of Human Sciences* 1 (1988): 47–73.

Subsequent art historians contested Burckhardt's thesis concerning the Italian origins of Renaissance naturalism. In Belgium, for example, it was Hippolyte Fierens-Gevaert, writing at the beginning of the twentieth century, who first insisted that the origins of naturalism could be traced back to Flemish artists of the fourteenth and fifteenth centuries.[19] Ironically, the claim that naturalism was a Flemish invention proved the downfall of Memling's exalted position in the canon. In the eyes of Fierens-Gevaert, it was the style of the Flemish primitives, rather than the content of their art, that had lent them their historical power. In an interpretive scheme governed by teleology, it was predictable that the innovative naturalism of the van Eycks should come to be regarded as more important than the spiritual sentiments of Memling. According to Fierens-Gevaert, the van Eyck brothers were the architects of early Netherlandish painting. The Adam and Eve panels from the *Ghent Altarpiece* (figs. 2 and 3) became valued for their remarkable fidelity to nature, rather than for their role within the theological program of the whole work.[20] In the context of the world-historical importance ascribed to van Eyck, Memling's star began to pale and fade. Fierens-Gevaert's evaluation of the Memling paintings included in the famous *Flemish Primitives* exhibition held in Bruges in 1902 was devastating.

> Ecstasy is demanded in the presence of the paintings of this charming master, and on this occasion it has become frenzied. Alas, I have not been able to share this premeditated enthusiasm. The great artist appeared affected next to van Eyck, artificial next to van der Weyden, without precision next to Thierry Bouts, without sobriety next to Gérard David.[21]

19. Hippolyte Fierens-Gevaert, *La Renaissance septentrionale et les premiers maîtres de Flandres* (Brussels: van Oest & Co., 1905). Fierens-Gevaert followed the lead of the French art historian Louis Courajod, who had argued that the origins of artistic naturalism should be traced to France because it was in the French courts of the Dukes of Berry and Burgundy that Flemish artists had initiated their naturalistic experiments (see Haskell, *History and Its Images*, 444). For a much fuller account of the relation between naturalism and nationalism in art historical scholarship on early Flemish painting of the nineteenth century, see Krul, "Realisme, Renaissance en nationalisme."

20. Fierens-Gevaert, "L'Exposition des primitifs flamands à Bruges," *Revue de l'art ancien et moderne* (1902): 110.

21. Ibid., 177. "L'extase est de rigueur devant les tableaux de ce maître charmant et, cette fois, elle est devenue de la frénésie. Hélas! je n'ai pu partager cet enthousiasme prémédité. Le grand artiste m'a paru mièvre à côté de van Eyck, artificiel à

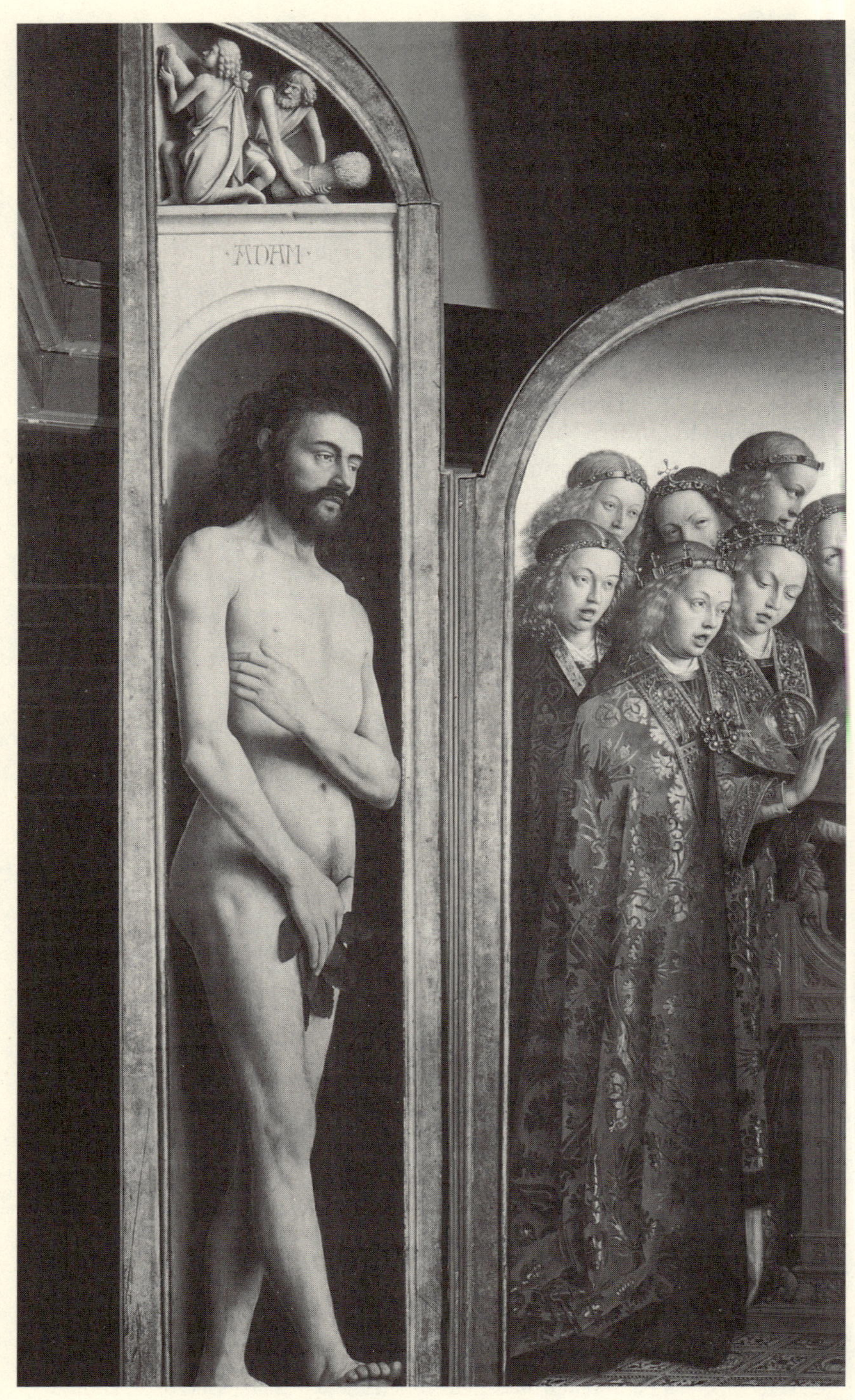

2. Jan van Eyck, *Adam* (detail from the *Ghent Altarpiece*), 1432. Oil on wood. Cathedral of St. Bavo, Ghent. Courtesy of Scala/Art Resource, New York.

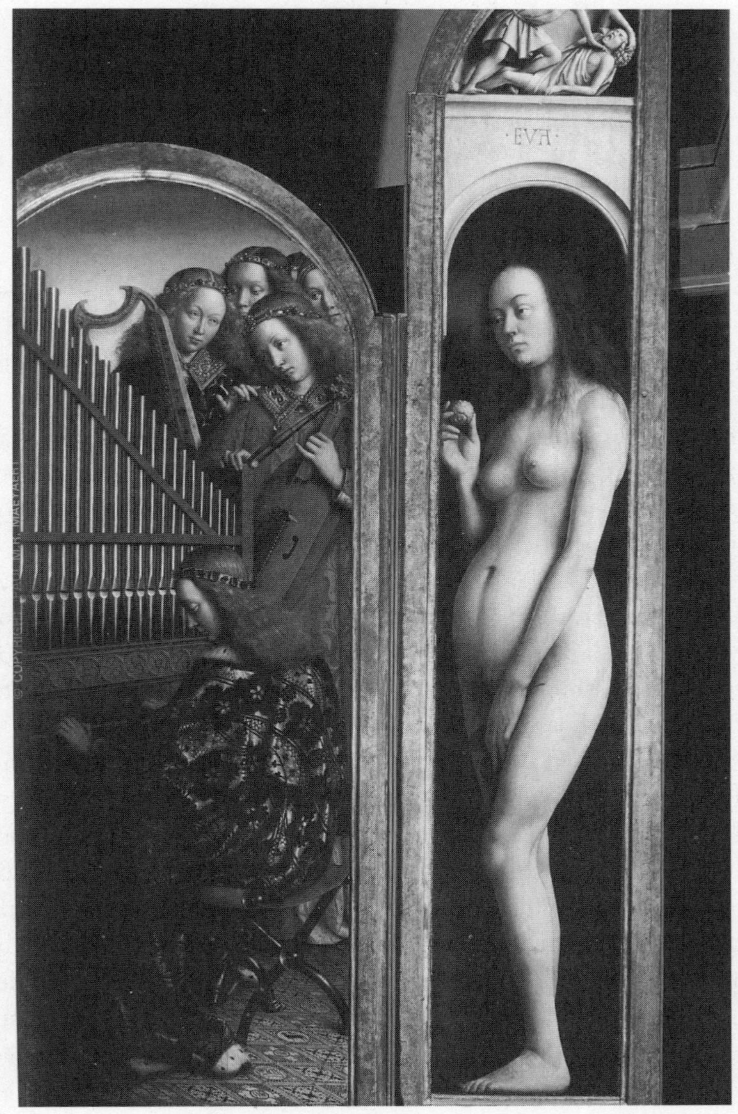

3. Jan van Eyck, *Eve* (detail from the *Ghent Altarpiece*), 1432. Oil on wood. Cathedral of St. Bavo, Ghent. Courtesy of Scala/Art Resource, New York.

Fierens-Gevaert's remarkable self-reflexivity in formulating these judgments offers us an interesting insight into a transitional moment in the history of taste.

> Nevertheless, I confess that for the past few years I have not felt as keenly the religious passion which is usually attributed to the illustrious master Hans. I scarcely have acknowledged this change to myself; I fought against that which I regarded as a weakness in my taste. Today, I admit that Memling no longer has, in my eyes, the exceptional importance or the creative grandeur not only of a van Eyck, but even of a Roger van der Weyden, a Gérard David or a Quentin Metsys.[22]

The triumph of the history of art as a history of style, as well as the triumph of the Renaissance at the expense of the period that preceded it, meant that Memling's spirituality could not now be identified with the progressive workings of the spirit. The forward march of history replaced the nostalgia of the romantics for the lost piety of a bygone age. History no longer simply looked back, but looked back in order to see the future. Religious devotion had no place in a scheme leading to the unfettering of human consciousness and its return to the natural world. Historians no longer daydreamed about the past as a way of validating the present, but about the utopian ambitions of the moment—ambitions that were inextricably identified with the politics of the emerging nation-states.

Predictably, Max Friedländer, director of the Kaiser Friedrich Museum in Berlin and architect of the canon of early Netherlandish painting still observed by scholarship today, did not support Fierens-Gevaert's claim that naturalism was a Flemish invention. Far from viewing it as a historical development in which Flemish artists just happened to play a major role, Friedländer believed that naturalism was a characteristic of the German people (a widely held conviction that can be traced back at least as far as Gustav Friedrich Waagen's influential monograph of 1822 on the van Eyck brothers).[23] Writing in the context of World War I, Friedlän-

---

côté de van der Weyden, sans rigeur à côté de Thierry Bouts, sans sobriété à côté de Gérard David."

22. Ibid., 177–78. "Toutefois, j'avoue que depuis quelques années je sentais s'amoindrir la passion religieuse qu'il est convenu de vouer à l'illustre maître Hans. J'osais à peine m'avouer à moi-même ce changement; je luttais contre ce que je croyais une faiblesse de mon goût. Aujourd'hui, je confesse que Memlinc n'a plus à mes yeux l'importance exceptionelle et la grandeur féconde, non seulement d'un van Eyck, mais même d'un Roger van der Weyden, d'un Gérard David, d'un Quentin Metsys."

23. Gustav Friedrich Waagen, *Ueber Hubert und Johann van Eyck* (Breslau: Josef Max & Co., 1822), 145. See also Wilhelm Waetzoldt, *Deutsche Kunsthistoriker*

der emphasized that the naturalism of early Flemish artists was indebted to their Germanic background: "Apart from personal genius that triumphantly transcends place and time, we may regard as Germanic heritage the impulse to observe nature that bears such fruit throughout Eyck's work and confers universally acknowledged superiority on Netherlandish panel painting."[24] Friedländer's stress on the German character of Netherlandish naturalism echoes Schlegel's failure to differentiate between German and Netherlandish national identity. The physical contiguity between German and Netherlandish territory, the similarity between the German and Dutch or Flemish languages, and the history of shared religious and political institutions allowed German scholars of Friedländer's generation to include Netherlandish culture within the parameters of what was considered the broader concept of German identity.

Friedländer was not the first to argue that naturalism was an essentially Germanic characteristic. Wilhelm Worringer, for example, had claimed in 1912 that it was the fusion of the abstract, linear quality of the spiritual art of the German Middle Ages, together with the mimetic tradition of Italian art in the work of German artists of the Renaissance, that produced the greatest achievements of naturalistic art in the Western tradition.[25] Friedländer's Austrian contemporary Max Dvorák also argued that naturalism was a special characteristic of the German people. In an ingenious argument that turned the tables on the Hegelian association of the observation of nature with the Italian Renaissance, Dvorák insisted that the Renaissance and the Middle Ages were far from standing in a dialectical relationship with one another. Rather, the Renaissance represented the fruition of Gothic naturalism that was the supreme quality of the art of the Middle Ages. Not only did naturalism originate in the art of the Middle Ages rather than in the Renaissance, but it was also the product of the northern European

---

(Berlin: Hessling, 1965), 38–45, and Gabriele Bickendorf, *Der Beginn der Kunstgeschichtsschreibung unter dem Paradigma "Geschichte." Gustav Friedrich Waagens Frühschrift "Ueber Hubert und Johann van Eyck"* (Worms: Wernersche Verlagsgesellschaft, 1985). For a critique of the nationalism of German art historical scholarship in the period between the world wars, see Pierre Francastel, *L'Histoire de l'art: Instrument de la propagande germanique* (Paris: Librairie de Medicis, 1945).

24. Max Friedländer, *From van Eyck to Bruegel* (London: Phaidon, 1969), 5.

25. Wilhelm Worringer, *Form in Gothic*, trans. Herbert Read (New York: Schocken, 1957), 59–67.

peoples rather than those of the Mediterranean.[26] While Dvorák's argument takes issue with Burckhardt's identification of realism with the Renaissance, thus breaking with Hegel's assessment of the age's historical significance, his own interpretation substitutes another transcendental narrative for the one he contests. Escaping the Hegelian tradition in one regard, his own story has a developmental structure, one that privileges the notion of the evolution of style, and therefore belongs to a pattern made popular by teleological historicism.

Regardless of whether it was nation or race that prompted Friedländer to reclaim Flemish painting for the Germanic people (or, as seems more likely, some combination of the two), the assertion is once again motivated by the prestige of naturalism's identification with the Renaissance as an age that saw the rise of individualism: "The naturalism of the new pictures is closely related to the growth of individualism. Tradition has begun to loosen its hold, eyes were trained on the world's infinite diversity—and rigid contemporary patterns lost their power."[27] The emphasis on style is structurally related to the neglect of content. Where stylistic innovation is absent, devotional subject matter is regarded as hackneyed and conventional. According to Friedländer, Memling does not participate in the naturalistic observation that characterizes the school to which he belongs. His art is said to depend on that of his predecessor Roger van der Weyden, whose compositional formulae he repeated without alteration. Memling failed, in other words, to behave like an exemplary "Renaissance man." "Whether or not Memlinc had a personal relationship with Rogier, whether or not he spent any time in the Brussels Workshop as an assistant or journeyman, his was an almost womanly receptivity in respect of the actively creative Netherlander. Memlinc was conquered and he never quite liberated himself."[28]

26. Max Dvorák, "Die Geschichtliche Stellung Huberts und Jans und das Geheimnis der Neuen Kunst," in *Das Rätsel der Kunst der Brüder van Eyck* (Munich: Piper Verlag, 1925), 141–242.

27. Friedländer, *Early Netherlandish Painting*, vol. 1, *The van Eycks—Petrus Christus*, trans. Heinz Norden, with comments and notes by Nicole Veronee-Verhaegen (New York: Praeger, 1967), 19.

28. Friedländer, *Early Netherlandish Painting*, vol. 6a, *Hans Memlinc and Gerard David*, trans. Heinz Norden, with comments and notes by Nicole Veronee-Verhaegen (New York: Praeger, 1971), 32.

Friedländer's gendering of Memling as female is meant to signal his failings as an artist. Both the Kantian notion of the genius as an extraordinarily gifted individual and Hegel's concept of the world-historical "hero" (such as Napoleon), a figure who transcends the culture of his time in order to bring about the next chapter in the history of the spirit, had been gendered male. By identifying Memling as female, Friedländer consigned him to the ranks of minor masters. As such, he was clearly regarded as an unworthy vehicle for a nationalist history of art. His alleged passivity also affects Friedländer's understanding of Memling's spirituality, so that his piety is now regarded as naively sentimental.

> In Memlinc's devout vision, acceptance knew no struggle, dedication no doubts, no ecstatic crises. He saw the world of God in a state of paradise, as an assemblage of pure beings, their bliss best exemplified by pleasing forms. His creatures are accessible—there is no arrogance about them. Shy and coy at first, they later relax into smiling security and animated trust, bringing more and more brightness into the gloomy churches of Flemish towns.[29]

Friedländer's evaluation of Memling's oeuvre was closely followed by the most authoritative twentieth-century historian of the northern Renaissance, Erwin Panofsky. In Panofsky's work, Memling is accused of failing to exercise his powers of observation in the representation of nature (a quality that Panofsky also identified with the northern races and with the Flemish people in particular),[30] is faulted for his dependence on Roger van der Weyden, and is dismissed as a *retardataire* rather than a progressive figure in a narrative propelled by the inexorable march of history toward the glorious dawn of the Renaissance.[31] As we have seen, the fact that Memling's work is so closely related to that of Roger van der Weyden was an important reason for granting him a minor role in the history of early Netherlandish painting. Both Friedländer and Panofsky, for example, suggest that his incapacity to develop a distinctive style of his own is an index of his lack of artistic talent. This

29. Ibid., 34.
30. Erwin Panofsky, *Early Netherlandish Painting*, 2 vols. (Cambridge: Harvard University Press, 1953). For an example of his identification of naturalism with the Flemish people, see 1:53.
31. Ibid., 1:347–50.

incapacity also implied that Memling should not be associated with the new age of the Renaissance, which, since Burckhardt, had been identified as the age of "man and the rediscovery of the world."

The ignominy of Memling's failure to live up to the expectations of Renaissance individualism was exacerbated by his comparison with his contemporary, Hugo van der Goes. At first sight, the importance ascribed to Hugo's work seems paradoxical, for his work is also marked by symbolic and mystical qualities that openly compromise the "reality effects" produced in his paintings. Yet the key to Hugo's location in the canon has less to do with his participation in the stylistic development that led to the Renaissance than with his identification as an artist who personified the quality of freedom characteristic of the new age. Whereas the Hegelian narrative usually equates naturalism with artistic genius, in Hugo's case these concepts are contrasted to one another. Hugo's ability to transcend the principles of the art of the Renaissance—reminiscent of the struggle of the Hegelian dialectic—establishes him as a personality who is bound neither by place nor by time; he embodies, in other words, the individualism of the age of the Renaissance. The depiction of Hugo as a Renaissance man, moreover, suggests a desire to show that during this period the appearance of artistic genius was not limited to the Italian peninsula.

The exceptional nature of Hugo's personal history was crucial to the Hegelian project of identifying him as a northern manifestation of Renaissance genius. Unlike Memling, about whom the romantic myth of his having been a soldier who sought shelter in the Bruges hospital of St. John in order to be cured of his wounds—and who had subsequently painted the altarpieces that still grace this institution out of gratitude to the nuns who tended him[32]—was soon dispelled for lack of documentation, Hugo was unremittingly linked to an even more lurid biographical tale. The story of Hugo's mental illness and retreat into a monastery at the height of his career could be substantiated in the archives, and the record of his troubles, kept

32. Biervliet, *Leven en Werk*, 112. Biervliet traces the story to Jean Baptist Descamps's *La Vie des peintres flamands, allemands et hollandais* (Paris, 1753). It colors the rather dissolute characterization of Memling in the popular 1859 English historical novel by Charles Reade, *The Cloister and the Hearth: A Tale of the Middle Ages* (New York: Grosset and Dunlap, 1922).

by one of the brothers of the cloister, was published in the earliest monograph on the artist by Alphonse Wauters in 1872.[33]

Wauters developed the romantic potential of the story, speculating that Hugo's despair was caused by the conflict between the ascetic aspirations that had led him to the monastic life and his longing for the sensuality and dissipation of an earlier existence.[34] Early-twentieth-century art historians, however, under the spell of a teleological approach to history, found it easy to identify his malady as an outbreak of melancholy, the mental condition of Renaissance genius. Friedländer, for instance, writes:

> Van der Goes, Grünewald and Michelangelo—three artists of melancholic temperament. Aside from the works that testify to the somber moods of their authors, there is no dearth of confirmatory evidence to show that in these men blackness of soul transcended the normal limits of the healthy mind.[35]

The state of Hugo's mind thus accounts for the nature of his art; his individualism is woven into the fabric of the Hegelian dialectic of the Renaissance and the Middle Ages. He is claimed to belong to a transitional moment, one in which the medieval guild system was breaking down. Though the regulations and requirements of the guilds still determined artistic production, Hugo proves the exception to the rule. For Friedländer, he is the artist who breaks the bonds of convention and is ahead of his time.

> The virtues compatible with the guild system were virtues anyone could acquire—hard work, honest craftsmanship. They did not include genius, the kind of extraordinary skill that sets its owner apart, exalts him, marks him as someone special. It was fame that burst the confines of craft society. A master who grew aware of his superiority, who perceived the difference between his work and that of his colleagues as a gulf that could not be bridged, became an enemy of society, felt like an intruder in the community.[36]

33. Alphonse Wauters, *Hugo van der Goes. Sa Vie et ses oeuvres* (Brussels: Hayez, 1872).
34. Ibid., 22.
35. Friedländer, *Early Netherlandish Painting*, 6a:48.
36. Ibid., 6a:50.

The condition Wauters had described as a personal struggle between two sides of Hugo's personality, an allegory of the battle between the spiritual and the sensual, becomes heroic, replete with social and transhistorical significance in Friedländer's vivid account. Hugo personifies the Hegelian spirit, torn between the ambition to express his genius and a desire for a self-effacing piety.

> Pride, ambition, the joy of creating were at war with his religious qualms, his need to humble himself. His visions, his spiritual experiences, were at odds with pictorial tradition. The art that was born of these inner struggles attained grandeur and pathos. . . . He was a stranger in Ghent, a stranger in the monastery, a stranger to his age. Striding forward in solitude, he lost his way. No wonder we associate him with Grünewald and Michelangelo—two who came later than he.[37]

Friedländer's prose suggests the aesthetic rewards to be obtained from subscribing to the Hegelian paradigm. His poetic evocation of Hugo's inner conflict, the struggle between the piety of the dying Middle Ages and the self-assertiveness of the pagan Renaissance, clothes Hugo's mental distress in a striking series of metaphors that serves to make his art memorable to us. In a figure such as Hugo, the history of art as a history of style reaches its fruition. The meaning of history is suddenly exposed as transhistorical forces clash and contend with one another in a dialectic that gives rise to the future.

Panofsky, author of the definitive study on Renaissance melancholy,[38] again followed Friedländer in his account of Hugo's work. He attempted to add historical texture to this art historical narrative of the rise of Renaissance individualism by indicating that the Renaissance doctrine of the melancholic genius was first laid out by Marsilio Ficino in a book published in 1482—the year of Hugo's death.[39] This coincidence, however, possesses more power on the metaphoric level than on the historical. Panofsky admits, for example, that there was little interaction between the cultures of Italy and the Netherlands during the fifteenth century and that

37. Ibid.

38. Panofsky and Raymond Klibansky, *Saturn and Melancholy: Studies in the History of Natural Philosophy* (London: Nelson, 1964).

39. Panofsky, *Early Netherlandish Painting*, 1:330.

the humanist ideology on which Ficino's thesis depends was wholly foreign to Hugo's Ghent. Panofsky's argument betrays the desire to find a manifestation of Renaissance genius in a culture to which such an idea was manifestly alien, a need to name Hugo a northern equivalent to personalities such as those of Leonardo, Raphael, and Michelangelo. If the artistic autonomy and power asserted by such artists could be understood in terms of the psychological theories of Ficino, then so could Hugo's.

Like Friedländer, Panofsky reads Hugo's works as manifestations of genius. The scale of the figures in the *Portinari Altarpiece* (fig. 4)—a work that is said to be more at home in Florence, where it is now located, than in Ghent, where it was produced—is interpreted as a metaphor of Hugo's status as a *totus homo*, the fully realized "Renaissance man." Because of Hugo's transitional position—the fact that he appeared in a culture that had no way of recognizing the world-historical importance of his talent—he was necessarily conflicted, torn between "the humanistic glorification and idealization of man and the non-humanist principle of total particularization. . . . between 'great form' and the minutiae of optical appearance."[40] In an analysis that moves from the works to the artists and back again, Panofsky claims that Hugo's paintings are riven by contradiction. Of his last work, *The Death of the Virgin* (fig. 5), Panofsky eloquently writes:

> In the "Death of the Virgin," . . . the indistinct bleakness of the light that comes from the left foreground is shattered by the glare of the miraculous apparition while the desaturated blues, reds, mauves, pinks and browns, some of them as dissonant as unresolved seconds, weirdly contrast with the chalk-white of the Virgin's kerchief and St. Peter's alb and with the green-fringed yellow of the big glory. And the intensity of simple-hearted devotion, prophetic ecstasy and muted sorrow have reached a point at which emotion blots out consciousness and threatens to break down the barrier that protects reason both from the subhuman and the superhuman.[41]

In the figure of Hugo van der Goes, we thus witness the birth pangs of a new age. The artist's struggle to give expression to a new

40. Ibid., 332.
41. Ibid., 338.

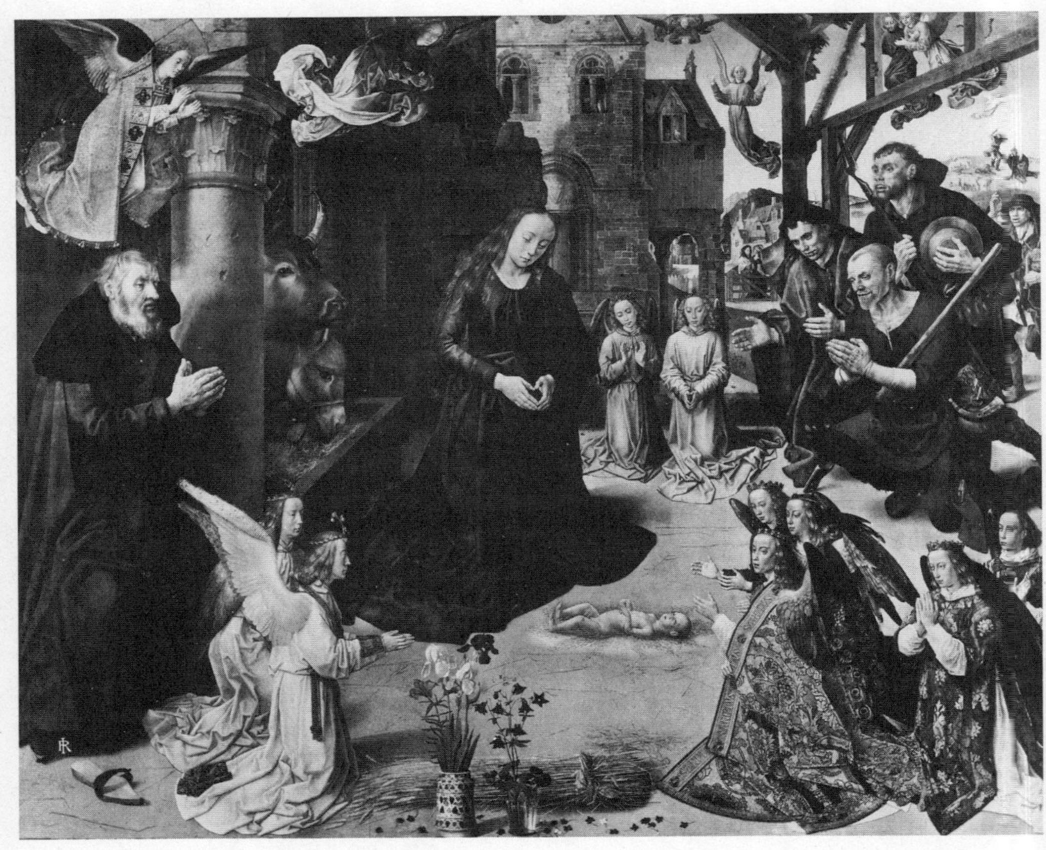

4. Hugo van der Goes, *The Adoration of the Shepherds* (center panel of the *Portinari Altarpiece*), ca. 1476. Oil on wood. Galleria degli Uffizi, Florence. Courtesy of Alinari/Art Resource, New York.

conception of human consciousness, one that depends on the capacity to realize his potential regardless of the limitations imposed on human conduct by historical (or national) circumstances, is responsible for his descent into insanity.[42] Memling, the copyist and follower of Roger van der Weyden, could clearly be no match for this eruption of Renaissance genius into the calm procession of early Netherlandish painting, a tradition which had until this point allegedly concerned itself with the rather pedestrian task of imitating nature.

42. For a critique of the equation of genius and insanity in art history, see Griselda Pollock, "Artists' Mythologies and Media Genius, Madness and Art History," *Screen* 21 (1980): 57–96.

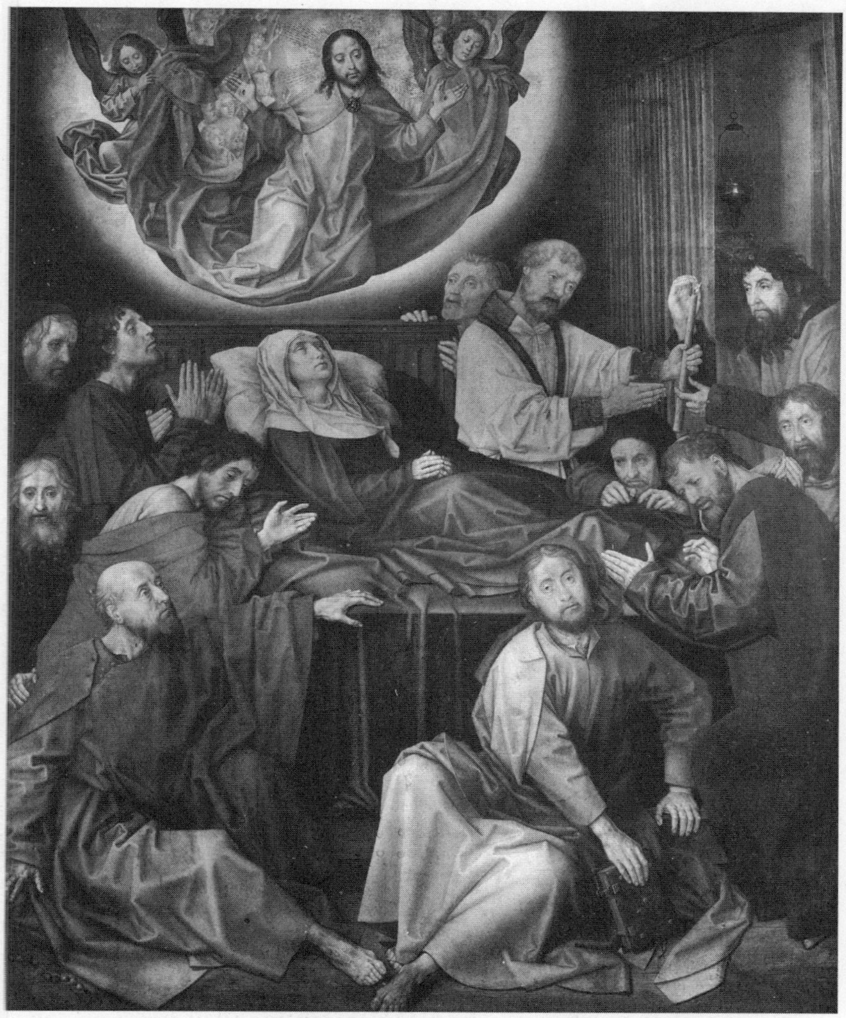

5. Hugo van der Goes, *The Death of the Virgin*, ca. 1481. Oil on wood. Municipal Museum, Bruges. Courtesy of Alinari/Art Resource, New York.

The superimposition of Hegelian teleology onto the romantic conception of the artist-as-genius adds status not only to the artist, the object of interpretation, but also to the historian. Identifying the life of Hugo van der Goes as a site at which it is possible to discern the workings of the spirit, the historian becomes a seer, someone who functions to explain the present in terms of the past. The spirit animates both Hugo van der Goes and the narrative of the historian. Historical authority is enhanced as the historian becomes the temporary embodiment of a world-historical process. The distance that distinguishes two historical horizons is erased in the voice of History itself.

The first objection to this teleological evaluation of Memling's artistic status and historical significance is found in Ludwig von Baldass's book of 1942.[43] Baldass outlines Memling's prominent place in the canon of Netherlandish painting, at least in the popular imagination, and contrasts it to the low esteem in which the artist is held by contemporary art historians. He claims that historians have preferred complex, difficult, and changeable artists over those whose work is simple, unproblematic, and peaceful. More important, Baldass argues that such historians should have been less willing to sacrifice the reputation of an artist who does not fit some preconceived notion of historical development.

> The historiography should not have as its only goal to move as fast as possible from Dirk Bouts and Hugo van der Goes in order to attain Geertgen and Quentin Metsys by placing the resolution of the problem of passionate expressivity and enhanced naturalism in the forefront of attention. In such circumstances any prolonged engagement with Memling's art appears like an unnecessary halting place.[44]

Writing in 1971, the English scholar K. B. McFarlane pursued Baldass's attack on the transcendental narrative that had condemned Memling to second-rate status, even obscurity.[45] He defends the pacific quality of Memling's art, suggesting that art need not disturb or unsettle in order to be deemed great. He mocks the language of Panofsky, who had, for example, called van Eyck an "explorer" and van der Weyden an "inventor," saying that such terms are an expression of the "Agonistic Ascendancy" in the histo-

43. Ludwig von Baldass, *Hans Memling* (Vienna: Schroll & Co., 1942).

44. Ibid., 7. "Zweitens darf die Geschichtsschreibung nicht nur das Ziel im Auge haben, so schnell wie möglich von Dirk Bouts und Hugo van der Goes zu Geertgen und Quentin Metsys zu gelangen und die Verfolgung der Probleme leidenschaftlichen Ausdrucks und gesteigerter Naturwiedergabe in den vordergrund des Interesses zu stellen. Dann erschient nämlich jede eingehende Beschäftigung mit Memlings Kunst leicht wie ein unnützer Aufenthalt."

45. K. B. McFarlane, *Hans Memling*, ed. Edgar Wind and G. L. Harris (Oxford: Clarendon Press, 1971), 38–45.

riography of this period.[46] He satirizes the assumption that only the artists who can be characterized as heroes, those involved in a dramatic struggle, deserve the attention of the historian. McFarlane is particularly concerned with the role that the notion of "progress" played in the Memling scholarship.

> This whole-hearted reliance upon what to others may seem a coarse identification of "progress" with "innovation," and preferably dramatic innovation, allows Memling's claims upon our attention to be quickly disposed of. He was retarded when he should have been advancing; he ought more obviously to have gone one better than his predecessors. . . . To equate novelty with life is to adopt a needlessly philistine solution to every historian's inescapable problem: how to distinguish the significant from the trivial. No mere rule of thumb can relieve him from the need to exercise his own judgement and consider pictures, like other historical "facts," on their merits.[47]

In conclusion, then, and in contrast to the nationalistic conflicts that raged about the origins of pictorial naturalism—conflicts that depended on Hegel's notion of the state as the embodiment of the spirit—the opposition of Hugo van der Goes and Hans Memling refers to another aspect of Hegel's thought. In Hugo van der Goes, Friedländer and Panofsky discerned a world-historical figure responsible for preparing the next stage in the history of the spirit. In doing so, they found a means by which the status of genius might be bestowed upon a "Germanic" artist, thus dignifying the northern tradition with the type of prestige that had hitherto been reserved for the Italian Renaissance. This strategy also allowed them both to account for the historical changes that distinguish sixteenth- from fifteenth-century Flemish painting. Hugo becomes the hinge on which the door of the new century swings open.

Many aspects of the contemporary approach to the work of Hans Memling have been prefigured by the imaginative contributions of the early-twentieth-century writer Johan Huizinga. In his

46. Ibid., 39.

47. Ibid., 44. McFarlane's criticism of the teleological bias of the Memling literature was also noted by Hull, *Hans Memlinc's Paintings*, 217.

influential book, *The Waning of the Middle Ages* (1924),[48] he forcefully rejects the idea that naturalism is somehow associated with national identity and that it relates to the rise of the Renaissance. In a compelling account of Franco-Burgundian culture of the fourteenth and fifteenth centuries, Huizinga proposes that far from being a harbinger of things to come, the naturalism of the art of this period is a symptom of a civilization in decline. Religious ideas had become ossified and meaningless, and as a consequence they could be rendered in material terms. The sparkling sensuality of the natural record in the art of Jan van Eyck, an art meant to please the tastes of his aristocratic patrons, was at odds with the intellectual and emotional significance of the religious subjects he represented.

> Instead of heralding the advent of the Renaissance, as is generally assumed, this naturalism is rather one of the ultimate forms of development of the medieval mind. The craving to turn every sacred idea into precise images, to give it a distinct and clearly outlined form, . . . controlled art, as it controlled popular beliefs and theology. The art of the brothers van Eyck closes a period.[49]

More important, in arguing that there is nothing exclusive about the naturalism of the Renaissance (pointing out that the observation of nature is a characteristic of the art of widely different periods, as well as a stylistic feature that often occurs in conjunction with styles characterized by idealization and abstraction), Huizinga suggests that this style cannot be associated with the artistic production of any single race or nation.[50] Furthermore, he notes, if we are to judge a style by its most developed manifestations, then it can be argued that naturalism is a feature of fifteenth-century Italian art rather than that of the sixteenth, where the movement is commonly said to have reached its apogee: "The essence of the Renaissance lies in its triumph over naive naturalism, and it is the fail-

48. Johan Huizinga, *The Waning of the Middle Ages: A Study in the Forms of Life, Thought, and Art in France and the Netherlands in the XIV & XV Centuries* (Garden City, N.Y.: Doubleday & Co., 1954).

49. Ibid., 264.

50. Huizinga, "Renaissance and Realism," in *Men and Ideas: History, the Middle Ages, and the Renaissance*, trans. James Holmes and Hans van Marle (New York: Meridian, 1959), 288–309.

ure to understand this that has led to the mistaken incorporation of Jan van Eyck in the Renaissance."[51]

In a remarkable reflection on the nature of visual mimesis, Huizinga argues that the terms *naturalism* and *realism* (he uses them indistinguishably) often refer to works which, while not actually corresponding optically to any particular set of natural circumstances, are nevertheless designed to give the impression that they duplicate the real world. His insight thus raises the prospect that naturalism may frequently create what Roland Barthes was later to call a "reality effect."[52] Huizinga's analysis allows for the possibility that the style which contemporary art historians were calling "Renaissance naturalism," a metaphor for the turn of the spirit toward nature, is actually nothing but the effect of a cultural value with ideological goals that may well transcend the principle of imitation.

If Huizinga and those who have followed him can be said to have broken the identification of naturalism with both the Renaissance and national identity, his understanding of the cultural significance of style nevertheless remains indebted to the teleological tradition. In comparing artistic production to rhetorical figures and social rituals, Huizinga, like Hegel, implies that each aspect of a particular culture is related to every other aspect of that culture, and that there is a process or development that unites them all. Huizinga's interpretation, in short, can still be regarded as an illustration of Hegel's wheel. Poetry, music, court etiquette, and visual art are all said to share certain qualities which are related to an explanatory thesis that accounts for the period as a whole, as the spokes of a wheel are related to its hub. While Huizinga's abandonment of style as the vehicle for the historical unfolding of the spirit represents a remarkable critique of the Hegelian tradition in art history, his work—in subscribing to Hegel's wheel—is still joined to a teleological historicism on a deeper and ultimately more problematic level. He remains confident that the Hegelian notion of the *Zeitgeist* (or "spirit of the times"), thought to pervade all aspects of each synchronic slice of teleologically conceived historical time, is suffi-

51. Ibid., 303.
52. Roland Barthes, "The Reality Effect," in *French Literary Theory Today*, ed. Tzvetan Todorov, trans. K. Carter (Cambridge: Cambridge University Press, 1982), 11–17.

cient to explain the relation of each individual manifestation of a culture to every other.

The effectiveness of Hegelian concepts as heuristic devices continues to be demonstrated in the Memling literature to this day. Writing in 1990, Paul Philippot, for example, makes use of Sixten Ringbom's thesis that Flemish painting of the fifteenth century represents a transition from iconic or devotional art to one that is concerned with the narrative aspects of the Christian story.[53] Memling's figures are said to lose their specificity as they share their ontological status with the depicted nature that surrounds them. Instead of freezing time for devotional purposes—reducing, say, the landscape setting to a backdrop for the motionless, eternal figures that were the objects of worship—Memling is said to forfeit some of that emotional intensity in an effort to endow the figures with an animated engagement with the circumstances in which they are represented. As the figures become less iconic, their relation to their surroundings becomes more active, and a devotional art is replaced by a narrative one. The viewer is encouraged to look and recognize, rather than worship.

Philippot attempts to rescue Memling from his devaluation at the hands of a narrative that exalted the rise of the Renaissance by writing him into one about the emergence of narrative art. Effective as this resuscitation is as a means of insuring that critical attention does not dismiss Memling out of hand, Philippot's account is teleological in nature. His Memling, torn between a devotional and a narrative art, is recuperated as the link that guaranteed the development of one into the other. It is the tension resulting from Memling's heroic intervention, from his attempt to mediate mutually antagonistic principles, that is said to mark his art as exceptional.

Conversely, in the literature on Hugo van der Goes, Bernhard Ridderbos has sought to interpret the artist's changing style in terms of the historical culture of which he was a part, rather than as a manifestation of the passage of the spirit.[54] Ridderbos returns to

53. Paul Philippot, "Icône et narration chez Memling," in *Pénétrer l'art. Restaurer l'oeuvre* (Kortrijk: Groeninghe, 1990), 77–84. This line of interpretation was originally proposed by Sixten Ringbom, *Icon to Narrative: The Rise of the Dramatic Close-Up in Fifteenth-Century Devotional Painting* (Abo: Abo Akademi, 1965).

54. Bernhard Ridderbos, *De melancolie van de kunstenaar. Hugo van der Goes en de oudnederlandse schilderkunst* (The Hague: SDU Uitgeverij, 1991).

a romantic reading of the artist's idiom as an allegory of his personal struggle between a desire for worldly recognition and a desire for spiritual redemption. Style, in other words, is not regarded as a transhistorical process in which the artist is the means by which the spirit manifests itself in history; it is an integral part of the work's social function. Like Huizinga, Ridderbos looks around the edges of Flemish naturalism to determine its cultural significance. Though he does not deny that the naturalism of van Eyck served a religious purpose, making transcendental truths materially accessible, Ridderbos believes that like Roger van der Weyden, Hugo sought to develop a style that was related to the spiritual agenda of the leading form of lay spirituality of his time, the *devotio moderna*. In doing so, Ridderbos relates two different aspects of Netherlandish culture, suggesting that their participation in a common *Zeitgeist* constitutes a historical interpretation. According to Ridderbos, Hugo's spiritual concerns prompted him to abandon the Eyckian idiom on which his reputation was established in favor of a more direct and passionate style that was calculated to appeal to the emotions of the beholder. Instead of illustrating the conflict between the Middle Ages and the Renaissance, as Panofsky suggested, Hugo's art is said to manifest the internal turmoil resulting from the artist's aspirations to social prominence and his need to prepare for his life after death. As in the older literature, both Philippot and Ridderbos purport to "find" their interpretations in the historical context they study and make use of Hegel's wheel in one form or another. In the case of Philippot it is found in the diachronic axis of the developmental narrative that traces the change from a devotional to a narrative art form; in the case of Ridderbos it is located in the synchronic movement that links Hugo's art to the devotional culture of his time.

In conclusion, this analysis of a segment of the art historical canon, the historiographic reception of the work of Hans Memling, has allowed us to meditate upon the way in which the history of art has been "framed" by a teleological historicism. While the individual subjectivities of historians ensure that history continues to provide us with everchanging accounts of the past, their contributions inevitably share certain philosophical assumptions. Such assumptions dictated that Memling's work should be evaluated in terms of a historical narrative that depended on the notion of style as a developmental process, one that achieved its apogee in the Renaissance. Hegel's account of the unfolding of the spirit in history, appropriated by nineteenth- and twentieth-century discourses of nationalism, enabled art historians to wrangle about the national origins of naturalism. The power attributed to individual artists as agents of historical change is another Hegelian conviction with a tenacious afterlife. From this angle, history becomes an allegory of the freedom of the humanist subject to determine his or her fate. The irony lies in the fact that "genius" only becomes evident as it realizes a thesis or brings closure to a narrative projected back into the past by the historian. The exceptional power of genius as a tool in the unfolding of the spirit lies in the artist's historical role, one retroactively assigned to him (less often to her) by the present.

And most important, perhaps, this discussion has allowed us to reflect upon what could be considered one of the "deep structures" of narrative history, namely, Hegel's wheel. In criticizing the Hegelian assumptions that have determined the nature of the stories told about the past, I do not mean to repudiate the desire to find meaning in that past. Mine is a call neither for history that eschews the ambition of strong interpretation nor for history based on allegedly neutral descriptions of empirical "fact." Some of the finest pages of art history—those produced by the founders of the discipline, Alois Riegl, Max Dvorák, Heinrich Wölfflin, Wilhelm Worringer, and Erwin Panofsky (who all saw in the principle of style a way of tracking the progress of the spirit in history) or those written by art history's Marxist wing, such as Frederick Antal, Max Raphael, Arnold Hauser, and T. J. Clark (who secularized and materialized the spirit as the class struggle)—are the products of the Hegelian tradition.

The difficulty presented by Hegelian histories lies not so much in the diachronic and synchronic axes of interpretation, for some such heuristic devices will be invoked in any form of interpretation, so much as with the historical horizon in which they are allegedly situated. Whereas the Hegelian historian naturalizes the authorial perspective by claiming insight into the immanent meaning of history, an interpretive gesture that suggests a correspondence between a sequence of events and the narrative that recites them, historians informed by poststructuralist theory can make no such claim. If we accept the conclusion that history's narrative cannot coincide with the events of the past, then it is no longer possible to situate the axes of interpretation in the historical horizon that is the object of study. Although both Hegelian and non-Hegelian histories can be told only from a position in the present, this chapter calls for an awareness of the historian's implication in the cultural politics of his or her own time. The historian must accept that the patterns discerned in the past serve the cultural, ideological, and often nationalist needs of the present.

CHAPTER TWO

History, Fiction, Memory

Riemenschneider and the Dangers of Persuasion

> a remembrance is in very large measure a reconstruction of the past achieved with data borrowed from the present, a reconstruction prepared, furthermore, by reconstruction of earlier periods wherein past images had already been altered.
>
> —Maurice Halbwachs, *The Collective Memory*

Why return to the issues of history's relation to fiction and memory? Have not several generations of philosophers of history—most notably, in this country, Hayden White, Robert Berkhofer, and Peter Novick—explored the consequences of the "linguistic turn" for historical writing, suggesting that far from being a transparent and a value-free encounter with the past, it inevitably wraps the past in the preoccupations of the present?[1] Has not the work of such theorists as Michel Foucault on power relations or Jacques Derrida on the metaphysics of language demonstrated that history's dependence on linguistic systems of signification means that this form of writing necessarily manifests the ideological commitments of its authors?

It is, perhaps, the peculiar juncture at which the discipline of art history currently stands that occasions a return to these issues. Having experienced a "theory revolution" in the 1980s, art historians seem to be experiencing a nostalgia for a simpler and happier age. Rather than a desire to acknowledge that art history's discourse is colored by the subject positions of those who participate in it, there seems to be a longing for a foundationalist epistemology, for a time when all authors are expected to write with one voice—even if that voice represents the interests of only a specific

1. See chapter 1, n. 1.

class, gender, and race. The point of resisting this impulse to return to a less conflicted moment in art history's past—the re-enactment, rehearsal, and re-performance of arguments that opened the doors to the recognition of different forms of subjectivity in the production of knowledge—is to defend the value of the interpretive opportunities that have been opened up by feminism, queer theory, and postcolonialism.

A classic strategy of those eager to challenge historians who recognize the role of language in veiling, rather than revealing, the past has been by reference to the Holocaust. How, it is argued, is it possible to suggest that historical accounts do not render the "reality" of the events of the past? Does this not open the doors to those whose politics leads them to deny that a mass extermination of European Jews took place during World War II? If language is said to mediate all relation to the past, does this not reduce history to rhetoric rather than elevate it to a search for the truth?[2]

This chapter deals with the Nazi historiography on the sixteenth-century German sculptor Tilman Riemenschneider in order to explore the dangers as well as the opportunities afforded us by approaching history as a form of persuasion. My interest in Riemenschneider's historiography was sparked by an exhibition of his work held at the National Gallery in Washington, D.C., and later at the Metropolitan Museum in New York during the fall and winter of 1999–2000. One of the things that struck me about this exhibition, particularly as it was installed in Washington, D.C., was the "white cube" aesthetic that informed its presentation.[3] Sculptures lit by spotlights were placed on pedestals against stark grey walls. Although any exhibition of Riemenschneider's work must inevitably suffer from the fact that his monumental carved altarpieces cannot be moved from the churches in which they are located, it still seemed unfortunate to me that the works were displayed with such willful disregard to their original function. Their transformation from works of devotion to works of art was completed by the "tombstone" wall labels that, apart from author,

2. See, for example, Tony Judt, "Writing History, Facts Optional," *New York Times*, 13 April 2000, A31.

3. For the ideological significance of this concept, see Brian O'Doherty, *Inside the White Cube: The Ideology of the Gallery Space* (Santa Monica, Calif.: Lapis Press, 1986).

subject, and medium, limited themselves, by and large, to comments on the artist's stylistic development. Far from seeking a presentation of this work that would heroize the artist's dramatic life, I had hoped for some acknowledgment of the complexity of the cultural moment in which the sculpture was produced. Riemenschneider was, after all, caught up in the Peasants' War of 1525 and had been imprisoned and tortured for his membership in the Würzburg town council, a council that had forsaken its allegiance to the prince-bishop (whose castle overlooked the city) in order to side with the rebels. In addition, his sculpture was produced at a time when decisive challenges were being made to the form of religious piety that his sculpture represented. None of this tumult and conflict, however, was registered in the exhibition's display.

The exhibition's catalogue addresses a broader range of issues. Essays describe the historical context of the artist's activity, the quality of his carving technique, his preference for monochrome rather than for the more conventional polychrome sculpture, and an overview of the reception of his work in the historiographic literature.[4] Specialists are thus afforded a richer spectrum of interpretation than is the general public, whose experience of Riemenschneider's art remains unsullied by nonaesthetic considerations.

How had art historical knowledge managed to sanitize the objects of its study to such an extent that the vital role played by these sculptures in the production of religious and cultural meaning could be overlooked? A review of the literature on Riemenschneider soon revealed that the artist's life and work had been the object of varied historical interpretations, some of which were political in nature. I became intrigued by the fact that these interpretations were relatively unknown. It was as if art history had suffered amnesia when it came to Riemenschneider's treatment by German authors during the Weimar Republic. What follows, then, is an attempt to understand the reasons that prompted this oblivion, as well as to reflect upon the implications of this for our conception of the nature and status of historical writing.

Georg Dehio's four-volume history of German art, written during World War I, sets the tone for much of the subsequent writing

4. See *Tilman Riemenschneider: Master Sculptor of the Middle Ages*, ed. Julien Chapuis, exhibition catalogue (Washington, D.C.: National Gallery of Art, 1999), 119–42.

by German art historians on the same subject.[5] Dedicated to his three sons, who are said to be either soldiers on the western front or Allied prisoners of war, Dehio declares that his study is not just an account of art produced in Germany, but also a service to the German people. It is they, the German people, who are to be regarded as the true heroes of his narrative. Drawing a distinction between scholarship that is restricted to empirical information and *Bildung*, by which the individual achieves cultural refinement through education, Dehio claims that in studying German art, Germans can come to know themselves.

What is it that Germans might discover about themselves in the art of the past? What essential characteristics of the nation can be revealed by works of art? Part of Dehio's answer is a response to the challenge leveled at German art history by the French scholar, Emile Mâle, in a series of articles published in 1914. Mâle argues that all German art was plagiarized from the art of other nations. Using the notion of originality, which had been raised to the status of an absolute value by art theorists and historians of the nineteenth century, Mâle claims that Germans had always been imitators rather than innovators.[6] Dehio responds that Mâle's criticism depended on a mistaken conception of originality. Even the greatest genius, he writes, cannot create something out of nothing. The true genius of the German people always has been to take ideas from others and to improve upon them.[7]

More profoundly, Dehio finds that German nature is filled with a sensitivity for the unbounded and incomprehensible nature of Being. To the German, the Renaissance clarity of forms appears to be a beautiful lie. Dehio argues that for the German, dissonance, not harmony, is the essence of existence, and that he therefore prefers art that is unclear, indefinite, and uncontained. Rather than admire realized Being, it is the surge of Becoming with which he is

5. Georg Dehio, *Geschichte der deutschen Kunst*, 4 vols. (Berlin: Walter de Gruyter, 1919–26). For an overview of the work of some of the authors who contributed to a nationalist conception of German art, see Hans Belting, *The Germans and Their Art: A Troublesome Relationship*, trans. Scott Kleager (New Haven: Yale University Press, 1998).

6. Emile Mâle, *L'Art allemand et l'art francais au moyen age* (Paris: Lux, 1917). For a French reaction to the nationalism of German art history during the interwar period, see Pierre Francastel, *L'histoire de l'art: Instrument de la propagande germanique* (Paris: Librairie de Medicis, 1945).

7. Dehio, *Geschichte der deutschen Kunst*, 1:vi.

said to identify. While German nature is attracted to the classical on the basis of reason, it is in the Gothic, the romantic, and the baroque that it can abandon itself to the primordial power and depth of its instincts.[8]

This vision of the study of German art as a specifically national enterprise, one committed to the examination of art and artists with whom native bonds can be claimed, was a feature of German art historical scholarship during the Weimar Republic. For my purposes, the author most relevant to Riemenschneider's historiography in the Weimar period is, undoubtedly, Wilhelm Pinder.[9] Pinder compares the role of German scholarship to a military general staff. Just as it is the duty of the officer corps to bring out the unique capacities of the German soldier, so the German art historian must make the art of the past meaningful to the contemporary experience of the German people.[10] The soldier does not understand the work of his superior officers any more than the layman understands academic research. Yet the work of the scholar is crucial to the welfare of the people. Without historical inquiry, some of the leading manifestations of German national identity, such as

8. Ibid., 3:177. The values attributed to German art by Dehio may have their source in Nietzsche. Kurt Karl Eberlein, however, quotes Nietzsche without providing a reference: "Just as everything loves its own likeness, so the German loves the clouds and everything that is unclear, in transformation, misty and concealed; he experiences as deep anything which is uncertain, unformed, shifting and changing. The German is nothing in himself, he becomes, he makes himself." ["Wie jegliches Ding sein Gleichnis liebt, so liebt der Deutsche die Wolken und alles was unklar, werdend, dämmernd, feucht und verhängt ist; das Ungewisse, Ungestaltete, sich Verschiebende, Wachsende jeder Art fühlt er als tief. Der Deutsche selbst ist nicht, er wird, er entwickelt sich."] *Was ist Deutsch in der deutschen Kunst?* (Leipzig: Seemann, 1934), 26; my translation.

9. For an excellent analysis of Pinder's work in relation to the nationalist movements of his day, see Marlite Halbertsma, *Wilhelm Pinder und die Deutsche Kunstgeschichte* (Worms: Wernersche Verlagsgesellschaft, 1992).

10. Wilhelm Pinder, "Pflicht und Anspruch der Wissenschaft," in *Gesammelte Aufsätze* (Leipzig: Seemann, 1938), 214. Pinder's view of the social function of the art historian may be indebted to Kurt Karl Eberlein: "The art historian is no specialist, but rather a figure of national significance: seer, expounder, interpreter all in one. He is not the connoisseur of the art market but the connoisseur of the spirit of art, of the national artistic and ethical values, of its artistic signs and its artistic language. He is the watchman and lookout, the teacher and defender of the state's art and its art politics." ["Der Kunsthistoriker ist kein Spezialist, sondern eine nationale Persönlichkeit, Seher, Deuter, Dolmetscher zugleich, nicht der Kenner des Kunstmarktes, aber der Kenner des Kunstgeistes, der nationalen Kunst-und Lebens-werte, der Kunstzeichen und Kunstsprache, Wächter und Warner, Lehrer und Wehrer des Kunstreiches und seiner Kunstpolitik."] See *Was ist deutsch*, 7. For

the paintings of Grünewald or the medieval sculpture known as the Bamberg Rider, would have remained unknown.

By this account, the scholar's role is to bring to memory the artistic accomplishments of the German past in order to inspire the German present. Pinder faithfully fulfilled this conception of the mission of the German art historian with his own multivolume survey of German art.[11] The preface to volume 3, for example, informs the reader that it is because the author is no longer capable of active service that the book should be regarded as his contribution to the war effort. Arguing that what is important about history is not empirical detail but the interpretation of its significance, he sets about to define the quintessentially German character of German art. The Germans, he asserts, have no reason to feel culturally inferior to other European peoples. It is only Germany's defeat in World War I that promoted this impression.[12] Far from being comfortable and cozy, as it is so often caricatured, German art is the art of the warrior—not that of the petit bourgeois. The German is a spiritual Viking whose spirit leads to the most vivid self-expression. Reason should only be regarded as a German quality if it acts as counterweight, a principle of moderation, on a drive that borders on the self-destructive.[13]

Pinder's conviction that it is the duty of the German art historian to interpret the past in light of the needs of the German people in the present is echoed in Hans Weigert's 1935 book, *The Contemporary Tasks of Art History*.[14] Weigert wages a frontal attack on the notion of art historical objectivity. To his mind, specialization and professionalization have occasioned the downfall of the history of art, for the specialist can only be a prosaic connoisseur, not a lofty hermeneut.[15] The Nationalist Socialist "revolution," however, provides scholarship with a goal, an end, and a purpose.

Pinder's relation to Eberlein, see Peter Betthausen et al., *Metzler Kunsthistoriker Lexikon* (Stuttgart: Metzler, 1999), 68.

11. Pinder, *Vom Wesen und Werden deutscher Formen*, 3 vols. (Leipzig: Seemann, 1935–40).

12. Ibid., vol. 1, *Die Kunst der deutscher Kaiserzeit bis zum Ende der staufischen Klassik* (Leipzig: Seemann, 1935), 30.

13. Pinder, "Veit Stoss," in *Gesammelte Aufsätze*, 186.

14. Hans Weigert, *Die heutigen Aufgaben der Kunstwissenschaft* (Berlin: Deutscher Kunstverlag, 1935).

15. Ibid., 40.

The art history of the future will serve the German people, for National Socialism offers a way to combine the will to truth with the will to service.

The charismatic program outlined by Pinder and Weigert proved highly influential. Fritz Knapp's 1936 book on Riemenschneider identifies the artist with what is most purely and quintessentially German.[16] For Knapp, his works offer the spectator access to the sensitivity of the German soul. Riemenschneider and Grünewald are to be considered the most expressive representatives of the late Gothic spirit. Unlike Dürer, who worked in Nuremberg, a cosmopolitan city with many foreign influences, Riemenschneider's art preserved its purity because it was created in a milieu that was exclusively German.

In Kurt Gerstenberg's book of 1941, Riemenschneider is characterized as an artist of the second rank.[17] His limitations, however, are also described as his strengths. The integrity of his artistic conviction was such that it prevented him from being affected by foreign influences. Even if this hermeticism placed certain constraints on his art, it nevertheless ensured its purity. Grounding himself on his own spiritual resources, Riemenschneider expressed the essence of the German national spirit, a trait that allowed him to produce "melodies" that "belong to the eternal heritage of the German people."[18]

Perhaps the most strident identification of Riemenschneider with the cause of German nationalism—one that expressly considers him as a heroic representative of the German race—is found in Max Wegner's monograph of 1937.[19] Regarding Christianity as inimical to the German race, Wegner considers it his duty to rescue

16. Fritz Knapp, *Riemenschneider* (Bielefeld: Velhagen and Klasing, 1936), 9.

17. Kurt Gerstenberg, *Tilman Riemenschneider* (Vienna: Anton Schroll, 1941). Gerstenberg's nationalist agenda had been established in his 1913 treatment of German Gothic architecture as a special development that was quite distinct from the history of this style in the rest of Europe. See *Deutsche Sondergotik: Eine Untersuchung über das Wesen der deutschen Baukunst in späten Mittelalter* (Darmstadt: Wissenschaftliches Buchgesellschaft, 1969). Gerstenberg's work is discussed by Lars Oloff Larsson, "Nationalstil und Nationalismus in der Kunstgeschichte der zwanziger und dreissiger Jahre," in *Kategorien und Methoden der deutschen Kunstgeschichte 1900–1930*, ed. Lorenz Dittmann (Stuttgart: Franz Steiner Verlag, 1985), 175.

18. Gerstenberg, *Riemenschneider*, 8.

19. Max Wegner, *Tilman Riemenschneider. Der deutsche Künstler und Rebell* (Landsberg: Pfeiffer, 1937).

Riemenschneider from the grasp of interpretations that characterize him as a pious man. Wegner's thesis is that the history of German art and culture has been distorted by the imposition of Christianity on northern Europe. The degenerate peoples of the Mediterranean are held responsible for forcing a Semitic, Near Eastern religion upon a race for whom its values were alien. The organic unity of German culture was broken by the propaganda of the Roman Church. The German unity of God and man was destroyed at the moment when God was raised to an inconceivable height and man reduced to something filthy and pitiful.[20]

Wegner sees the struggle of the Germans against Christian ideology as a constant in German art, one that reaches its climax in the Renaissance. Blinded by Italian art, Albrecht Dürer is held responsible for the collapse of the Gothic style in Germany. Riemenschneider, on the other hand, might just have transformed the Gothic into a German Renaissance if he had not fallen foul of the politics of the Peasants' War. The opposing forces of German race and Christian ideology resulted in an intolerable tension that Riemenschneider sought to resolve through his work. Again and again, he tried to break through the "foreign" (i.e., Christian) narratives he illustrated in order to express the racial imperatives that motivated him. This unconscious struggle, however, could find no resolution. Torn between his German blood and foreign subject matter, Riemenschneider could find no other way out of his existential predicament: he consequently turned his unsatisfied energy to the field of politics.[21]

Wegner interprets Riemenschneider's involvement in the Peasants' War as a commitment to the cause of German unification. Far from being a class struggle, Wegner argues, the war manifested the eternal desire of the German people to be politically united. Having tried and failed to reconcile the German and Christian traditions in his art, Riemenschneider now joined forces with those fighting for the resurgence of Germany as a political power. Though he eventually failed in the endeavor, his struggle, suffering, and longing are said to have been fulfilled in the era of National Socialism.[22]

20. Ibid., 10.
21. Ibid., 26.
22. Ibid., 29.

Although the record I have been describing dominated Riemenschneider studies during Weimar, any balanced account of the historiography of the period would have to mention the work of Justus Bier. Bier's publications on Riemenschneider span half a century. The first two volumes of his monograph appeared in 1925 and 1930, while the last two were published in 1973 and 1978.[23] It is, of course, Bier's work before World War II that interests us here, for his books may be considered the exception that proves the rule. Providing us with a detailed, careful analysis of Riemenschneider's style and iconography, his interpretation of the artist's involvement in the Peasants' War depends on his characterization of Riemenschneider as a profoundly devout believer in the reformed faith.[24] Far from siding with the peasants in an unsuccessful attempt to unify Germany, Bier argues, Riemenschneider felt repugnance for the courtly ways of the Catholic clergy and identified with the common man. It may be unnecessary to add that as a Jewish scholar, Bier was forced to flee Germany in 1937. He took refuge in the United States, accepting a position at the University of Kentucky, which he held until his death.[25] Perhaps his faith, his identity as a member of an increasingly despised religious minority, prevented him from subscribing to the nationalist tenor of Riemenschneider scholarship during the Weimar Republic.

As we have seen, Dehio's argument that German art had a distinct identity, one that separated it from the artistic production of other European states in the same period, along with his claim that the study of German art had special benefits for the fate of present-day Germans and Germany, established a program that was followed by many of his art historical successors. The notion of style is crucial to his definition of German national identity. Rather than in the classical aesthetic, it is in the restlessness of the Gothic, the romantic, and the baroque that the realization of German consciousness may be discerned. For Pinder and Weigert, the study of German art becomes a duty: an obsession with positivistic research of an empirical nature must not blind the historian from his responsi-

23. For the history of these publications, see Justus Bier, *Tilman Riemenschneider: His Life and Work* (Lexington: University of Kentucky Press, 1982), preface.

24. Bier, *Tilman Riemenschneider. Ein Gedenkbuch* (Vienna: Anton Schroll, 1938), 17.

25. For Bier's career in Germany and the United States see Till-Holger Borchert, "Shifting Critical Fortune," in *Tilman Riemenschneider: Master Sculptor*, 136.

bility to find patterns that are relevant to the demands of contemporary German history. Interpretation becomes all-important as art history is conceived of less as a discipline in its own right than one whose function is to serve the German people in the present. For Pinder, German art is the art of a warrior race, not just restless, but irrational and violent. Whereas Knapp and Gerstenberg had found Riemenschneider's sensitivity and purity to be emblematic of his Germanness, Wegner characterized his art as riven by a fierce internal struggle. According to Wegner, Riemenschneider's failure to reconcile the values of Christianity with the demands of his German heritage created an art that was anguished and tormented, and ultimately led him to a path of self-destruction in the context of the Peasants' War.

Before addressing the more general questions concerning history and its relation to fiction on the one hand and memory on the other, I must address the way in which Riemenschneider was written about by the novelists of National Socialist Germany. The fact that so many were drawn to write about him is provocative, and an analysis of how their accounts differ from those of art historians may elucidate the distinctions we continue to make between these literary genres.

The number of literary authors who based their work on Riemenschneider's life during the years immediately preceding and during World War II is striking. At least four different authors made him the subject of their novels between 1936 and 1938. The first of these, Felix Beielstein, paints a dark and violent picture of Germany in the early sixteenth century.[26] The country is described as lawless, broken up into innumerable feuding political entities, and torn by religious and class dissension. His narrative's leading theme is given in a vignette that enlivens the introduction. After describing the tolls charged on the transport of goods by every small administrative body in Germany, including those transported

26. Felix Beielstein, *Die Grosse Unruhe. Ein Tilman Riemenschneider Roman* (Braunschweig: Georg Westermann, 1936). Apart from the novels mentioned in the following text, I am aware of two others that I have not been able to include in this study. Nora Wydenbruck's 1939 *Gothic Twilight* (London: Westhouse, 1946), was kindly lent me by Professor Miles Chappell. A quick glance reveals it to be a historical romance that revolves around Riemenschneider's four marriages. The other, Leo Weismantel's 1936 *Dill Riemenschneider. Der Roman seines Lebens* (Berlin: Union Verlag, 1956), has much the same character.

across the bridges of Riemenschneider's own city of Würzburg, Beielstein describes an exchange that allegedly took place between the artist and one of the prince-bishops of Würzburg's tax collectors. Objecting to the payment of tolls, a truculent Riemenschneider wonders why anyone should be charged to transport goods from one part of Germany to another. The tax collector replies that he is simply looking after his own interest; is he to be quiet when all the rest of the world is shouting? The artist's exchange with the tax collector should be regarded as an allegory of his sympathy for the imperial cause, for he believes that self-seeking should stop and only one voice, that of the emperor, be heard.[27] If we substitute Adolf Hitler for the emperor, we can, I believe, decipher the main thrust of Beielstein's tale.

While there is a rich and colorful account of Riemenschneider's artistic activity—his troubles with the other members of the sculptors' guild, the Dionysian energy with which he throws himself into his work, and his unhappy love affair with a woman who is driven to enter a cloister because she resents his infatuation with his art—the hero of the novel is an aristocrat called Florian Geyer, a historical figure, who became one of the leaders of the peasant movement. Geyer, who is against tolls, petty bureaucracies, and local frontiers, is dedicated to the unification of Germany under the authority of the emperor. He is ultimately defeated by his nemesis, Johannes Wittstock, the representative of the prince-bishop, Konrad von Thüngen. In the closing pages of the novel, Geyer reflects that the defeat of the unification attempt can be blamed on the fact that circumstances were not ripe. He claims, however, that "the dream of the great uprising of all Germans cannot be forgotten."[28]

In Luise Bachmann's 1937 novel, Riemenschneider is cast in a decidedly different light. The sculptor, who is said to speak a Franconian dialect that is almost unintelligible as rendered in the text, is cast as a simple, good-hearted craftsman who is articulate in defense of German art. When told that in Italy no one sculpts wood anymore, but only stone or bronze, he reacts angrily. Why should wood not be used in the making of a sacred image? After all, wood

27. Beielstein, *Die Grosse Unruhe*, 14.
28. Ibid., 332.

was made holy for all time by Christ's death on the cross.[29] He goes on to attack the Italian Renaissance for the rules and regulations of its art theory, asserting that materials alone should determine the way in which they are handled. According to Bachmann's Riemenschneider, an artist's creative energy cannot come from anywhere but his own heart. The reference to Christ's death, however, is a clue to Bachmann's view of the artist. He emerges from her story as a kind of secular saint.

There is, of course, plenty of time to inform us about Riemenschneider's love life, especially his closeness to one of his stepdaughters, a sentimental attraction which, after the death of his first two wives, eventually results in marriage. In an interesting twist, Bachmann makes Hans Bermeter, the populist agitator who involved Riemenschneider in the opposition to the prince-bishop during the Peasants' War, another of Riemenschneider's stepchildren. This invention intensifies the drama, making Bermeter's betrayal of Riemenschneider all the more poignant.

The story, however, revolves around Riemenschneider's piety, sympathy for the poor, gradual conversion to the reformed cause, and self-sacrifice in supporting the peasants. In the description of his arrest, with which the novel ends, Riemenschneider is reconciled to his fate because he has heard an inner voice reassuring him that his works will last long after his death.[30]

In Paul Arnold's novel of 1938, Riemenschneider is cast as an earnest craftsman who, on becoming convinced of the Lutheran message, sympathizes with the peasant cause.[31] His concern is said to be motivated as much by his desire for the unification of Germany as by religious faith. The freedom sought by the peasants—freedom of belief, freedom from serfdom, freedom to hunt—are all considered freedoms to be held under the authority of one lord, the emperor. These privileges, which Riemenschneider supports, are viewed as manifestations of an inexorable historical march toward social enlightenment.[32] Despite the piety ascribed to Rie-

29. Luise George Bachmann, *Meister, Bürger und Rebell. Das Lebensbild Tilman Riemenschneiders* (Paderborn, Vienna, Zürich: Schöningh, Fürlinger and Götschmann, 1937), 9.

30. Ibid., 391.

31. Paul Johannes Arnold, *Tilman Riemenschneider. Der Lebensroman eines grossen deutschen Meisters* (Berlin: Franz Eher nachf., 1938).

32. Ibid., 235.

menschneider, it is his involvement in the politics of German unification that is Arnold's main theme. Consequently, the tale must be regarded as yet another projection into the past of the ambitions of National Socialist Germany. Borchert, for example, has pointed out that in 1943 the novel was reprinted by the National Socialist Press in an edition of 42,000 copies.[33]

The most ambitious, complex, and thoughtful fictional account of Riemenschneider's life in these years is found in Karl Heinrich Stein's novel of 1936.[34] Published in Zürich—that is, in neutral Switzerland—it concentrates specifically on Riemenschneider's involvement in the events of the Peasants' War. The novelist locates Riemenschneider in a richly textured and historically informed account of the uprising. His analysis of the cultural and social circumstances of Germany in the early sixteenth century details the history of class warfare and the history of the dissemination of reformed ideas, as well as their interaction with one another. The uprising is thus characterized as a complex movement in which many different forces contend with one another.

Once more we read of Riemenschneider as a pious man who is profoundly moved by the Lutheran concern for social justice. Not only is the artist said to identify with the peasant class, but Stein also offers an interesting reading of his sculpture as accessible to peasant piety: his sculpted saints represent neither the gods of the rich nor the messengers of power and luxury, but rather embody the peasants' own humility.[35] Elsewhere, Stein suggests that the sculptor's bust of Würzburg's martyr, St. Kilian, could be understood by the reformed as the portrayal of an ordinary man, rather than a bishop (fig. 6). In characterizing the Saint as a servant of God, believers could strengthen their personal faith against those who had made a ritual of religion and in doing so served the cause of injustice on earth.[36] When Riemenschneider sees peasants praying to a sculpture of the Lamentation of Christ, he thinks that—far from being revolutionaries—they are the oppressed and persecuted, as well as his evangelical brethren.[37] The artist himself is de-

33. Borchert, "Shifting Critical Fortune," 141.
34. Karl Heinrich Stein, *Tilman Riemenschneider in deutschen Bauernkrieg. Geschichte einer geistigen Haltung* (Zürich: Buchergilde Gutenberg, 1938).
35. Ibid., 19.
36. Ibid., 146–47.
37. Ibid., 246.

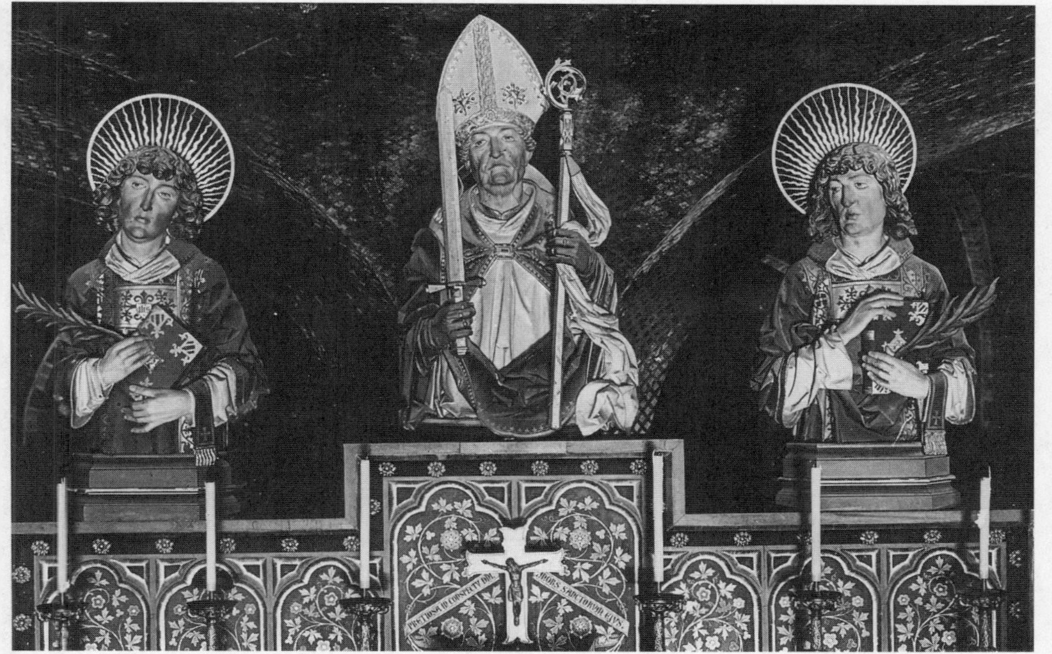

6. Tilman Riemenschneider, *The Three Franconian Apostles, including St. Kilian* (busts from the predella of the High Altar, Würzburg Cathedral; destroyed 1945), 1508–10. Limewood. Courtesy of Foto Marburg/Art Resource, New York.

scribed as working on a sculpture of the Lamentation for the town of Maidbronn when Würzburg is retaken by forces allied with the prince-bishop (fig. 7). Not only does Stein see this work as the culmination of Riemenschneider's artistic career—he believes that it represents the fruits of the artist's encounter with the art of the Italian Renaissance—but he also describes it as a document of Riemenschneider's personal feelings at the time. According to the author, the figure of the dead Christ embodies the anguish and despair of the artist's contemplation of the human suffering of his own time, the defeat of the peasants and the bloodbath that accompanied it. Because of the intensity of his emotion, Riemenschneider includes a self-portrait in the figure of Nicodemus who stands (holding an ointment jar) immediately behind Christ.[38]

38. For suport for this claim, see Corine Schleif, "Nicodemus and Sculptors: Self-Reflexivity in Works by Adam Kraft and Tilman Riemenschneider," *Art Bulletin* 75 (1993): 599–626.

The last, but by no means the least, literary figure to concern himself with Riemenschneider during the Second World War is none other than Thomas Mann. In a moving lecture given during his exile in the United States in 1945, Mann linked his own fate with that of the sixteenth-century artist.[39] In a wide-ranging discussion that explored the paradoxical nature of Luther's legacy for Germany, he chose to dwell on the reformer's attitude toward the peasants during the uprising of 1525. When the revolt (in large part inspired by Luther's teaching) began to threaten the status quo—frightening the secular and religious rulers of Germany—Luther saw his own cause endangered. Rather than see his religious revolution jeopardized by a secular one, he distanced himself from the peasant cause. Characterizing the peasants as misguided rebels who had misunderstood his ideas, Luther railed against them, encouraging the authorities to put down the rebellion by the most brutal means.

In Mann's opinion, Riemenschneider's heroism lies in his identification with the plight of the oppressed. In words that both resonate with his own convictions and mirror his own fate, he writes:

> moved by the great and fundamental contrasts of the time, he [Riemenschneider] felt compelled to emerge from his sphere of purely spiritual and esthetic artistic life and to become a fighter for liberty and justice. He sacrificed his own liberty for the cause he held higher than art and the dignified calm of his existence.[40]

Like Riemenschneider, Mann was forced to leave a life dedicated to contemplation as a consequence of his involvement in politics; his anti-Nazi position during the Weimar period resulted in his exile and loss of German citizenship. For Mann, Riemenschneider is the personification of the committed artist, the artist who is able to see beyond his own concerns enough to become involved in a fight for the common good. Riemenschneider, in the novelist's eyes, is the antithesis of Luther. Though the reformer had abandoned the

39. Thomas Mann, *Germany and the Germans* (Washington, D.C.: Library of Congress, 1945). The importance of this speech for Riemenschneider's historiography was recognized by Otto Schönberger, "Thomas Mann, Tilman Riemenschneider und Würzburg," *Mainfränkisches Jahrbuch für Geschichte und Kunst* 38 (1986): 188–89.

40. Mann, *Germany and the Germans*, 8–9.

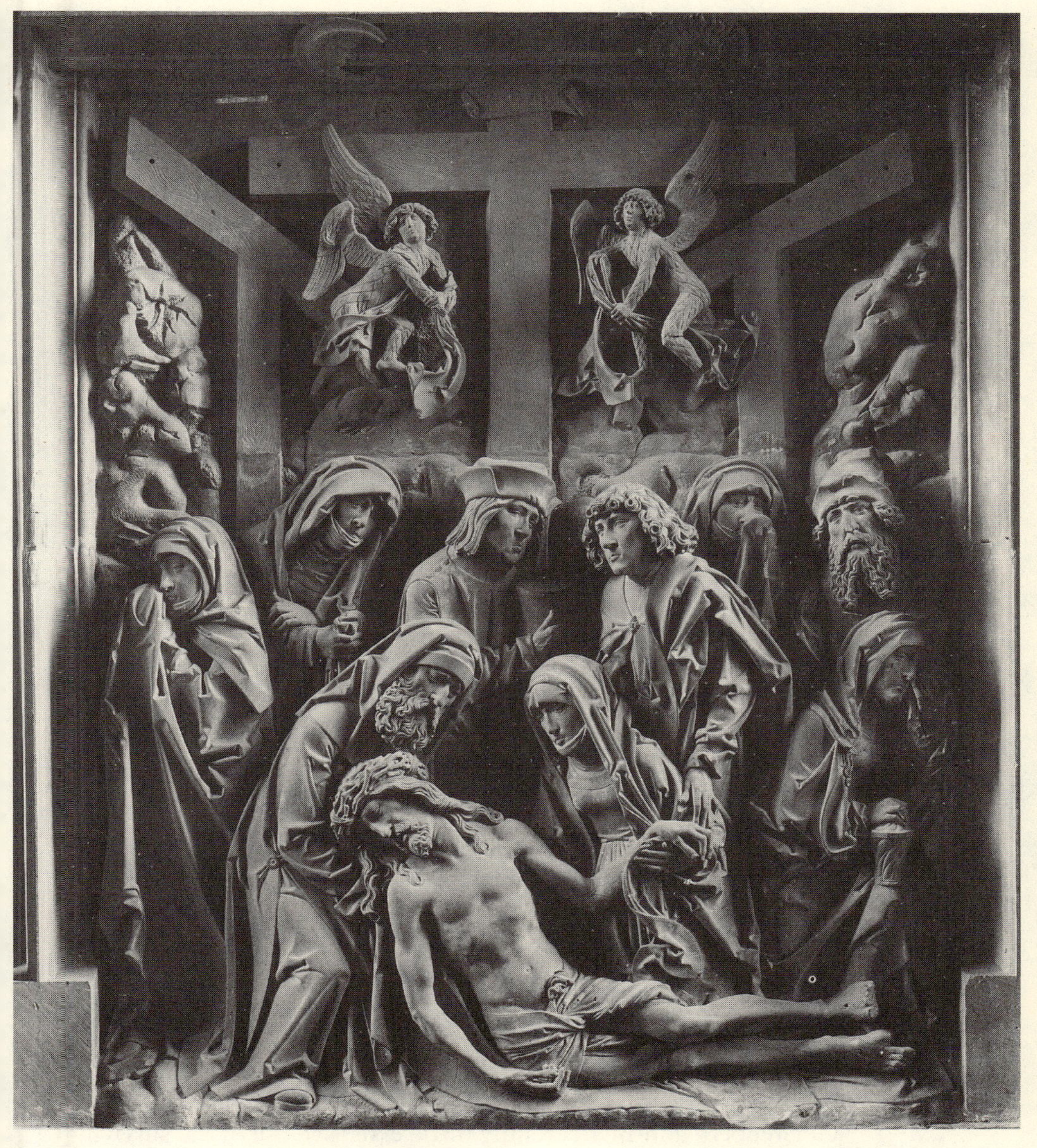

7. Tilman Riemenschneider, *Lamentation of Christ*, ca. 1519–23. Sandstone. Parish Church, Maidbronn. Courtesy of Foto Marburg/Art Resource, New York.

peasants in order to preserve his own cause, the artist abandoned his art for their sake.

Literary treatments of Riemenschneider during the National Socialist period suggest that novelists tended to interpret the significance of his life and work more variously than did art historians. Whereas almost all of the historians found in Riemenschneider's artistic style a manifestation of the eternal German spirit, writers of fiction used his life as an allegory not only of Germany's recent unification under its new political regime but also of Lutheran piety and a commitment to democratic values.

The nature of art historical writing during the interwar years may afford us some insight into this distinction. Art history's definition as a discipline dedicated to the study of the evolution of form, a principle that had enabled the field to become established as a legitimate member of the humanities, may also have been its most serious disadvantage. Most of the historians I have mentioned conceived of their task, first and foremost, as the chronicling of style. This bias in favor of the formal qualities of Riemenschneider's work meant that it was possible to neglect, or completely ignore, any reference to his life and times. An ahistorical concept of style played into the hands of those committed to an ahistorical conception of national identity. German nationalism—whether cultural or racial—depended on asserting an essential identity for the German people that transcended time and place. In divorcing style from history by equating it with the character of a particular people, some German art historians enabled their discipline to become part of a nationalist cause.

To what extent can the narratives about Riemenschneider told by art historians be regarded as any more or less fictional than those told by novelists? This is certainly not a distinction that can be settled on the basis of which group made greater use of the documents. Gerstenberg and Bier certainly made extensive use of the surviving historical record, but so did Beielstein, Bachmann, and Stein. Reference to the documents cannot thus be used to support one interpretation over another, let alone provide a criterion for distinguishing between art historical and literary writing. Indeed, those art historians most committed to the Nazi cause, such as Weigert and Wegner, expressly attacked the other art historians of their day for their allegiance to the positivist study of empirical evidence.

But there may be another basis upon which the history/fiction distinction can be maintained. Just as art historians have used style as the paradigm around which to construct their professional work, the novelists all seem to feature a certain tone and a number of common elements. All of them betray a romantic attitude toward Riemenschneider's artistic production, a sometimes prurient interest in his four marriages, and a concern with his piety and Lutheran conversion as well as his commitment to the cause of German unity. While some authors emphasize one dimension above another, these ingredients occur in almost all of the novels. The most, perhaps, that can be said—and that only tentatively—is that the art historians betray a more guild-like mentality. The notion that art history is about style clearly serves as the principle that holds the discipline together.

Is the nationalist attack on empirical research, the call for an interpretive rather than descriptive approach to art history, to be regarded as something pernicious and dangerous, or as the articulation of a false dichotomy? Historians today, who have by and large accepted that description *is* interpretation—that no account of the past can be entirely free of the value of the present—will find the Nazi distinction a spurious one. The National Socialist call for a history that responds to the political needs of the present, however, sounds more problematic. The arrant nonsense of an art historian who saw in Riemenschneider the clash of race and religion tends to set our teeth on edge. Yet we too search for contemporary language with which to make sense of events that transpired in the long-dead past.

One response to this dilemma, of course, is the one given by art history during its most scientific moments in the era following the Second World War. During this period, the heyday of iconography and social history, the historical horizons of past and present were rigidly separated. Historical interpretations deliberately repressed their entanglements in contemporary culture in order to obtain what was characterized as transparent access to the past. Panofsky's notion of "disguised symbolism," for example, proved an effective way of suggesting that the significance of late medieval paintings exceeded their apparent concern with mimesis. Armed with an encyclopedic knowledge of theology, the interpreter was allegedly able to discern religious symbolism lurking beneath the surface of apparently naturalistic representations.[41] Other strategies by which later historians sought to conceal the projection of contemporary values into their accounts of the past include T. J. Clark's concept of the "public," the unconscious spirit of an age that was only to be unlocked by the historian's quasi-psychoanalytic skill in understanding "the points at which the rational monotone of the critic breaks, fails, falters."[42] Similarly, Michael Baxandall's "period eye," a particular configuration of visuality that is said to determine the nature of artistic production, was only to be reconstituted by the painstaking labor of the historian.[43]

As we have come to realize, the attempt to insist upon an absolute distinction between the historical horizon of the interpreter and the historical horizon under discussion has proven untenable. The fetishization of the lost object of art historical desire, the concern to inquire only into the original intentional meaning of works of art rather than the significance of their ongoing reception, has had reductive implications for the process of interpretation. The insistence on the importance of different subject positions and the introduction of feminism, queer theory, and post-colonial studies have reminded us of the political stakes of the present's encounter with the past. Our reaction to the Nazi attack on empiricism should not therefore be a knee-jerk response in defense of positivism, but rather an acknowledgement that, whether we like it or not, the cultural significance of history writing lies in its rhetoric.

Rather than blind ourselves to the rhetorical potential of historical interpretation because of its abuse by the Nazis, I would argue that the past, in this case the life and work of Tilman Riemenschneider, offers the present an opportunity to articulate, by means of narrative, its potential for the ethical and political dilemmas we currently confront. The "constructedness" of historical interpretations assumed by this perspective cannot be discounted by recourse to the pejorative connotations of "fabrication." Once all historical narratives are acknowledged to meld past and present, to fuse ob-

41. Erwin Panofsky, *Early Netherlandish Painting*, 2 vols. (Princeton: Princeton University Press, 1953).

42. T. J. Clark, *Image of the People: Gustave Courbet and the 1848 Revolution* (Princeton: Princeton University Press, 1973), 12.

43. Michael Baxandall, *Painting and Experience in Fifteenth-Century Italy* (London: Oxford University Press, 1972).

jectivity and subjectivity, it is possible to accept that truth might not only be "found" but also "made."

Does the absence of a theoretical justification for claiming that one argument must be truer than another necessarily mean that "anything goes"? Is the Enlightenment's belief in reason an inalienable assumption of the human sciences? Must Nazi abuse of the persuasive possibilities inherent in all interpretation prevent the recognition of that potential today? The Nazi interlude in Riemenschneider scholarship is not something that is best avoided or forgotten in the interest of a naive ideal of scientific or value-free scholarship, but rather it should serve to remind us of the power with which political conviction can invest historical narratives. The fact that some of the strongest interpretations of the significance of Riemenschneider's life are associated with the powers of evil should not forever foreclose the possibility of strong readings that might serve very different forces in the present and the future.

On this point, I must be careful not to be misunderstood. Far from proposing a justification for Nazi models of history writing, this analysis of Riemenschneider scholarship during the era of National Socialism challenges the rhetoric once used to characterize his life and work. It does not do so, however, through reference to the "real"—to documents, archival material, and the like—for such material can serve a multitude of ideological purposes, as we have seen. Rather than suggest that the "facts" can prove an argument wrong, my point is that *all* historical writing is by definition an art of persuasion. One argument can only be countered with another. It is in this clash of rhetorics that historical insight is obtained, rather than through fruitless appeals to "what really happened."

These considerations bring me, finally, to my initial question regarding history and memory.[44] The interpretations of the past that we call history are those that have been filtered through the institutional screens of the present. These screens include the process

44. On this question see, for example, Maurice Halbwachs, *The Collective Memory*, trans. Francis Ditter Jr. and Vida Jazdi Ditter (New York: Harper and Row, 1980); Pierre Nora, "Between Memory and History: *Les Lieux de Mémoire*," trans. Marc Roudebush, *Representations 26* (1989): 7–25; and Patrick Hutton, *History as the Art of Memory* (Hanover, N.H.: University Press of New England, 1993).

of scholarly acculturation produced by university education, peer-reviewed publication, professional advancement, and so forth. As Karl Mannheim pointed out so long ago, these institutions function to ensure that there is a sociology of knowledge: that what counts as fact depends more upon historical circumstance than upon epistemological certainty.[45] History might therefore be characterized as that version of the past that the professional institutions of the present see fit to bequeath to the future.

The cautiousness of our contemporary situation, the positivism that still marks much art historical production, may well be regarded as a reaction against the abuse of history at the hands of the great totalitarian regimes of our century: National Socialism on the one hand, and state communism on the other. However salutary this disengagement from politics may appear in the light of the recent past, the historical disciplines may have paid too high a price for their "disinterest." In fact, art history's retreat to the ivory tower may well account for its fall from power as an influential discipline of the humanities. Whereas the nineteenth and early twentieth centuries could turn to art historians such as Heinrich Wölfflin, Alois Riegl, Panofsky, Max Dvorák, Wilhelm Worringer, Ernst Gombrich, Otto Pächt, Frederick Antal, and Arnold Hauser, for example, for sweeping meditations on the significance of images for our existential predicament, the same can rarely be said of the present.

My position is, of course, a paradoxical one. I seem to be arguing in favor of strong interpretations—that is, art historical works invested with powerful cultural and political argumentation—while at the same time calling the Nazi intervention into question. How, is it possible to argue against one form of strong interpretation and not others? The purpose in aligning some of the most distinguished contributions to our discipline along with some of the most questionable is not to suggest that they are somehow analogous, but rather to examine the assumptions that motivate them.

Art historians tend to assume that the history of art is an epistemological enterprise rather than a rhetorical one. The power, as

45. Karl Mannheim, *Ideology and Utopia: An Introduction to the Sociology of Knowledge*, trans. Louis Wirth and Edward Shils (New York: Harcourt, Brace and Co., 1936); for an interesting meditation on the status of historical "facts," see Michael Maranda, "Facts," *New Literary History* 29 (1998): 415–438.

well as the danger, inherent in this attitude lies in the way scholars naturalize their assumptions, their inclination to purport to find in the historical material the very significance they make of it. Far from denigrating the memory of some of the leading art historians of the past by invoking them in the same breath as their National Socialist epigones, I want to call attention to the status of their works as forms of rhetorical persuasion rather than descriptions of epistemological fact. This chapter seeks to bring to consciousness our capacity to confuse a profound commitment to a particular view with the conviction that this view actually corresponds with the circumstances it purports to understand. The dangers of persuasion lie in our failure to recognize that the history of art is a rhetorical rather than an epistemological endeavor; indeed, they lie not so much in rhetoric's capacity to win others over to our own point of view as in its power to convince *us* that this point of view is the only necessary way of interpreting the material at hand. The implication of my position is not, of course, to equate a Panofsky reading with one of, say, Wegner, but to point out that whether we agree with one or the other, its "truth" can never be proven in terms of "fact." Disagreeing with some of the interpretations of Riemenschneider's work because they seem to serve a repugnant political agenda depends on *our* values and *our* beliefs, not on any appeal to the foundations of knowledge.

At this point, a critical reader might ask if this argument is fair, or indeed relevant, to the conditions under which art historical business is currently conducted. To what extent do practitioners still regard their enterprise as an epistemological one? Have not art historians long been convinced that theirs is a rhetorical occupation, concerned to persuade rather than to define? Others will have to decide whether my perception of disciplinary debates bears any relation to actual historical circumstances. As I see it, the point of the epistemology/rhetoric distinction in this text, after all, is not to describe a state of affairs so much as to persuade the reader that there are no longer convincing grounds for accepting the distinction as viable.

If, following Freud, we cannot recall the past without filtering it through the present, then the task of each generation of historians is to shape a collective memory that is invested with contemporary meaning. This commitment leads to the conclusion that art history is better regarded as a form of rhetoric, a rhetoric of persuasion, rather than an accumulation of insights that together contribute to some universal conception of knowledge.

This chapter means to test this contention against one of the most radical challenges to its thesis, namely, the National Socialist interlude in Riemenschneider studies. This account of nationalist scholarship serves as an allegory of the dangers of persuasion, dangerous not just because of its political message but because of our failure to accept its status as rhetoric. Once the writings of the German nationalists can be recognized as something other than foundational claims to knowledge, we are in a position to analyze their persuasive strategies for what they are and to acknowledge that our own interventions in the rhetoric of history must also be informed by ethical and political agendas. Rather than consign Riemenschneider's historiography to oblivion, it is possible to recall its danger in such a way as to inform our own historical interpretations with perspectives that counter the nationalist ones. Instead of attempting the impossible, instead of cleansing art history of all bias or contemporary commitment, instead of isolating the presentation of Riemenschneider's art in "white cube" installations that are alien to their own historical horizon, it may be possible to do justice to the complexity of cultural transactions that once animated these works, as well as to the complexity of the intersection of our values with those of the past.

The challenge of the past to the present, therefore, might be to ask whether we have fulfilled our function as the custodians of cultural memory. Have we brought the past to mind in such a way as to manifest the rich potential inherent in the narrative process, or have we purposively constrained and restrained our interpretations so as to be able to aspire to a value-neutral position? Once the distinction between rhetoric and fact has been called into question and the historian's implication in contemporary cultural processes acknowledged, then it seems possible to ask: does the significance we attach to Riemenschneider today adequately reflect not only the circumstances of his artistic production but also those in which we currently find ourselves?

CHAPTER THREE

Motivating History

Under historicism, which entailed the historical study of ancient and modern art as a new paradigm of historical experience, art history handed over lock, stock, and barrel its legitimacy as a medium for aesthetic, philosophical, or hermeneutic reflection.

—Hans Robert Jauss, "History of Art and Pragmatic History"

Fortunately we are presently rather far removed from the period of naïve scientificity during which subjectivity was considered to be the domain of illusion and objective knowledge to be the sole expression of truth. We know now that our subjectivity is not an illusion to be overcome, but rather that it is another part of reality, no less important than any other part.

—Josué Harari and David Bell, Introduction to Michel Serres, *Hermes: Literature, Science, Philosophy*

I begin with an anecdote.[1] One day I went searching for a book in Avery Library, the art library of Columbia University. This time, instead of looking at the shelves as mere supports for the volumes that contained the information I sought, I became aware that what I was looking at was the architecture (or archaeology) of a particular field of scholarly activity, namely, the study of northern Renaissance art. I was struck, in other words, by the physical presence of an aspect of our discipline's cultural imaginary.

The organization of the volumes arranged on the shelves, I realized, was at least as important as the knowledge within the weighty tomes they supported. Rather than the disturbing chaos that characterized the stacks in Borges's tale, "The Library of Babel," these books were organized according to an established pattern. But just what was the system behind their organization? Where did this pattern originate? (Was it any more comprehensible than that which inspired Borges's equally famous account of an ancient Chi-

1. For the function of anecdote in historical narrative, see chapter 6.

nese encyclopedia—an account cited by Michel Foucault?)[2] How did the category of "northern Renaissance art" come into being as a topic worthy of scholarly interest? Who or what had determined that there should be more books on certain artists rather than on others? What likes and dislikes, commitments and dismissals, do these choices betray? What values went into forming the configuration of books assembled there, and more importantly, what continues to keep those books in place?

The answer, of course, is the canon—that most naturalized of all art historical assumptions. Certain artists and certain works of art that have received the sanction of tradition are unquestioningly regarded as appropriate material for art historical study. Course syllabi are still arranged around artists who are deemed major figures, and the vast majority of publications is dedicated to a consideration of a select number of well-known "masterpieces." The purpose and function of privileging certain artists and works in this way are rarely questioned. Indeed, critical analysis of the esteem in which the canon is held is not regarded as belonging to art history proper but rather to aesthetics, a branch of philosophy, or to the criticism of contemporary art. For the most part, art history's disciplinary work is carried on as if there were no need to articulate the social function it is supposed to serve. The discipline's promotion and support of the canon are all too often still taken for granted. It is as if a consensus had been arrived at sometime in the past, foreclosing further discussion. The library shelves are the physical manifestations of this consensus, the embodiment of an established cultural practice.

In asking for a discussion of the purpose of art history's dedication to the canon, I hope not to be misunderstood. Mine is not a call for a valuation of works of art, not a plea for a more explicit ranking of canonical works, not a request that students be indoctrinated as to which artist is "better" than another. The problem, it seems to me, is that somehow the notion of "quality," that most subjective of judgments, is thought to be self-evident and unques-

2. Michel Foucault, *The Order of Things: An Archaeology of the Human Sciences* (New York: Random House, 1973), xv: ". . . animals are divided into: a) belonging to the Emperor, b) embalmed, c) tame, d) sucking pigs, e) sirens, f) fabulous, g) stray dogs, h) included in the present classification, i) frenzied, j) innumerable, k) drawn with a very fine camelhair brush, l) *et cetera*, m) having just broken the water pitcher, n) that from a long way off look like flies."

tionable. While some of us may dwell affectionately and pleasurably on certain predictable canonical artists and describe their works in glowing terms, there is usually no attempt to argue (or even think about) why one artist should be considered more worthy of study than another, or why certain moments and places in the history of artistic production should be privileged above the rest. As it stands now, the history of art could be described as an unacknowledged paean to the canon, and the intensity of this devotion can, perhaps, be measured by the professorial sobriety with which we accomplish this task.

The conviction underlying such attitudes—which continue to be widespread, if not prevalent in art history today—is the commitment to tradition. The canon of artists and works discussed in art history courses are those which were once found meritorious by previous generations of scholars responding to very different historical situations than those we currently occupy. Like Mount Everest, the works, the artists, and even the methodologies for interpreting them are simply there, and like mountain climbers, it is our mandate as art historians to ascend their peaks and sing their praises to future generations. In doing so, we often unwittingly engage in the unthinking reproduction of culture: reproducing knowledge, but not necessarily producing it. As a consequence, the discipline has often played a conservative role in a rapidly changing society.

The way to start speculating about how we came to this disciplinary moment might be to engage in a cultural history of the discipline, an examination of the classed, gendered, and ethnically marked values that have shaped its development. Such a historiographic survey, however, would range farther than I wish to go. Instead, what follows is a discrete, limited examination of what could be called the founding moment of the canon of northern Renaissance art, the historical point at which a discursive practice first formed around works of art produced in northern Europe in the fifteenth and sixteenth centuries. In other words, this is not a historiographic account of the origins and development of the appreciation of northern Renaissance art so much as an analysis of the political, religious, and emotional sentiments that prompted that appreciation.[3] The analysis is meant to be representative; the

3. For a more detailed sketch of the appreciation of early Netherlandish art in the eighteenth and nineteenth centuries, see Francis Haskell, *Rediscoveries in Art:*

northern Renaissance is used here as a case study. (A similar review might also be undertaken for canonical artists and works of other times and places.)

Comparing the ideas that led to the historical study of the northern Renaissance at the end of the eighteenth century with those that informed the way in which the period was studied at the middle of the twentieth century, specifically in the work of Erwin Panofsky, allows us to analyze the role of the practice of history in two very different historiographic moments. How has the function of history changed in the period that separates the late eighteenth and the mid-twentieth centuries? Is there anything we can learn from the ways in which history has been conceived, something that might enable us to rethink the function of history writing in our own time?

Until the end of the eighteenth century, the discipline of art history, founded by Giorgio Vasari, remained focused on the humanist traditions of the Italian Renaissance as they were codified in the art academies of the seventeenth century. Not only were the styles and artistic techniques of the great masters of the Florentine and Venetian schools regarded as the models to which all artists should aspire, but the academies established a hierarchy of genres, according to which history painting—that is, the painting of religious and secular subject matter depicting lofty themes taken from Christian belief and Greco-Roman mythology and history—was ranked at the top, and mere exercises in mimesis—such as landscape and still life—were located at the bottom. Owing to the dominance of the humanist tradition among the European educated elite, there were few significant differences among the artistic aspirations of the schools of visual production that arose in regions that were later to become the major nation-states. Only in the eighteenth century was the dominance of the academy challenged by Johann Winckelmann, who proposed that the true source of beauty was to be found in the art of ancient Greece. Later, in the context of the national-

---

Some Aspects of Taste, Fashion, and Collecting in England and France (Ithaca: Cornell University Press, 1976); Suzanne Sulzberger, *La Réhabilitation des primitifs flamands, 1802–1867* (Brussels: Palais des Académies, 1961); and Bernhard Ridderbos and Henk van Veen, eds., *"Om iets te weten van de oude meesters." De Vlaamse Primitieven—herontdekking, waardering en onderzoek* (Nijmegen: Uitgeverij SUN, 1995).

ism engendered by the European wars that followed the French Revolution, arguments began to be fielded regarding the aesthetic interest of works of art produced at times and places other than ancient Greece and Renaissance Italy.

The first mention of northern Renaissance painting as a location for the discussion of artistic issues hitherto associated only with Italy and Greece is found in the curious and delightful writings of the short-lived young author, Wilhelm Heinrich Wackenroder. In his fictional *Confessions from the Heart of an Art-Loving Friar* (1796), Wackenroder makes a compelling case for the relativity of artistic appeal. In doing so, he boldly challenges the accepted canon of his day, according to which Italian art of the Renaissance and the Greek art of antiquity possessed greater merit than art produced at any other place and time.

> Stupid people cannot comprehend that there are antipodes on our globe and that they are themselves antipodes. They always conceive of the place where they are standing as the gravitational center of the universe,—and their minds lack the wings to fly around the entire earth and survey at one glance the integrated totality.
>
> And, similarly, they regard their own emotion as the center of everything beautiful in art and they deliver the final judgement concerning everything as if from the tribunal, without considering that no one has appointed them judges and that those who are condemned by them could just as well set themselves up to the same end.
>
> Why do you want to condemn the American Indian, that he speaks Indian and not your language?
>
> And yet you want to condemn the Middle Ages, that it did not build temples such as Greece?[4]

Wackenroder parades his appreciation for the art of the northern Renaissance in a chapter dedicated to the praise of Albrecht Dürer. His melodramatic account reveals the nationalistic and religious values that underlie his urge to insert this artist into the canon. Dürer is regarded as just as good an artist as those who constitute the canon because of the quality of his inner spirit, an inner spirit that represents the essence of the German nation.

4. Wackenroder, *Confessions and Fantasies*, trans. M. Hurst Schubert (University Park, Pennsylvania: Penn State Press, 1970), 109–10.

When Albrecht was wielding the paintbrush, the German was at that time still a unique and an excellent character of firm constancy in the arena of our continent; and this serious, upright and powerful nature of the German is imprinted in his pictures accurately and clearly, not only in the facial structure and the whole external appearance but also in the inner spirit. This firmly determined German character and German art as well have disappeared in our times . . . and the student of art is taught how he should imitate the expressiveness of Raphael and the colors of the Venetian School and the realism of the Dutch and the enchanting highlights of Correggio, all simultaneously, and should in this way arrive at perfection which surpasses all.—O, wretched sophistry! O, blind belief of an age that one could combine every type of beauty and every excellence of all the great painters of the earth and, through the scrutinizing of all and the begging of their numerous great gifts, could unite the spirit of all in oneself and transcend them all![5]

The encomium ends with the recounting of a dream in which the friar, having fallen asleep in an art gallery, has a vision in which artists come alive before their paintings and discuss their merits. The shades of Raphael and Dürer appear, whom the friar observes holding hands as they gaze in "friendly tranquility" and mutual admiration at each other's achievements. By pairing Raphael and Dürer in this way, of course, Wackenroder explicitly claims a heightened status for German painting of the Renaissance.

Wackenroder's argument concerning the relativity of artistic competence clearly depends upon the principle of historicism which had been introduced into the philosophy of history by Johann Gottfried von Herder a few years earlier.[6] Herder had argued that there could be no objectivity in the writing of history because

5. Ibid., 115.

6. See George Iggers, *The German Conception of History: The National Tradition of Historical Thought from Herder to the Present* (Middletown, Conn.: Wesleyan University Press, 1968), 34–38. The concept of historicism is subject to a variety of different definitions. See, for example, Maurice Mandelbaum, *History, Man, and Reason: A Study in Nineteenth Century Thought* (Baltimore: Johns Hopkins University Press, 1971). For an interesting attempt to dissolve the distinction between historicism and history by arguing that all histories share the kind of system-building quality usually attributed to historicist narratives, on the grounds that they are all structured according to rhetorical tropes, see Hayden White, "Historicism, History, and the Figurative Imagination," *History and Theory* 14 (1975): 48–67.

the historian was himself part of the historical process. For him, there are no transhistorical absolutes; all judgments are contingent upon the time and place in which they are produced. Wackenroder's artistic relativism—in particular, his claim that Dürer was the equal of Raphael—finds its basis in Herder's emphasis on the singularity of the historical moment. Wackenroder sees that the unique quality of a historical period, that which makes it unlike anything that preceded or followed it, can serve a national cause. The nationalism of the late eighteenth century, a moment when Germany sought to free itself from the political and cultural domination of France, found in the history of art a means by which its case might be articulated and advanced.

With Wackenroder's emphasis on the spirituality of art and its capacity to embody and transmit religious emotion, along with his conviction that these characteristics were to be found in the art of places and times that had not yet been hallowed by tradition, *Confessions from the Heart of an Art-Loving Friar* defined the romantic attitude toward the issue of artistic quality. Much the same tone is heard in the influential criticism of the writer Friedrich Schlegel, who, during a stay in Paris, was deeply affected by his experience of the Musée Napoleon. It was in the Louvre that Napoleon's artistic plunder, pillaged from all over Europe, was placed on view as an unprecedented display of imperial power.[7] Although Schlegel shared the admiration for Italian art typical of the taste of the day, he preferred the early painters of the fourteenth century. To his eyes their work exuded a greater spirituality. It was his affinity for the religious feeling of old master paintings that allowed him to extend his appreciation to what he called "old German" painting of the Renaissance, by which he meant not only German but Netherlandish art of this period as well.[8] Schlegel's advocacy of the virtues of old German painting soon drew the attention of the wealthy sons of a German businessman, Sulpiz and Melchior Boisserée, who traveled to Paris to meet him.[9] After staying at his house as

7. See Hans Eichner, *Friedrich Schlegel* (New York: Twayne Publishers, 1970).

8. Schlegel's views on art are found in Friedrich Schlegel, *Kritische Friedrich Schlegel Ausgabe*, vol. 4, *Ansichten und Ideen von der christlichen Kunst*, ed. Hans Eichner (Munich: Ferdinand Schöning, 1959).

9. For a history of the Boisserée brothers and their collection, see E. Firmenich-Richartz, *Die Brüder Boisserée: Sulpiz und Melchior Boisserée als Kunstsamm-*

paying guests, they traveled with Schlegel through northern France and the southern Netherlands, visiting Gothic cathedrals before returning to their native Cologne. In the account Schlegel later wrote of this pilgrimage, he identified the Gothic as the German style of the Middle Ages, extolling its beauties as manifestations of the age of faith.

Schlegel's views were symptomatic of a significant change of taste, one that ensured that his reevaluation of German art of the Renaissance would be underwritten by capital so as to eventuate in the formation of collections and museums. On their return to Cologne, the Boisserée brothers avidly began collecting German and Netherlandish art. Their passion was aided by political circumstances, for the Napoleonic expropriation of the properties of the Catholic church, enforced throughout occupied Germany as well as France, meant that medieval and Renaissance altarpieces that had been part of the neglected fabric of church interiors suddenly entered the marketplace in large numbers. The Boisserées soon assembled the largest and most important collection of paintings of this period, including some of the most admired works of Stefan Lochner, Roger van der Weyden, and Hans Memling. After having been made available to the Prussian crown, which was in the process of establishing what would eventually become the national museum in Berlin, this collection was eventually bought by the King of Bavaria in 1827, and thus found an alternative route to the fulfillment of Schlegel's call for a national museum of old German painting.[10]

Both Wackenroder and Schlegel, then, had used history as a means of realizing their critical appreciation of an art that was emotionally laden with religious values, an art which could consequently be appropriated as a glorious manifestation of the German national spirit. In this enterprise, they effectively laid the foundation for the study of what would come to be called northern Renaissance art. The legitimation of the history of northern Renaissance art continues to this day, but in radically different terms. I want to skip ahead a couple of centuries and examine how the

---

ler. Ein Beitrag zur Geschichte der Romantik (Jena: Diederichs, 1916) and Gisela Goldberg, "The History of the Boisserée Collection," *Apollo* (1982): 210–13.

10. Sulzberger, *Réhabilitation des primitifs flamands,* 57.

study of northern Renaissance art has been legitimated in the second half of the twentieth century. What kinds of stories about Netherlandish painting do we tell today and what motivates them?

The analysis of the twentieth-century discourse on northern Renaissance art is located in what is usually regarded as its apogee, namely, the work of Erwin Panofsky. Panofsky's book *The Life and Art of Albrecht Dürer* appeared in 1943, whereas *Early Netherlandish Painting* was published a decade later, in 1953.[11] Rather than using the past in the service of religious, emotional, and nationalistic goals, Panofsky's books appear to have no other ambition than to provide a wealth of information about the subjects under discussion. Both of his texts are detailed and learned readings of the available historical evidence, discussions that are, for the most part, pursued with a relentless "objectivity"—that is, with a positivistic desire to evaluate and supersede the nature and quality of the information given by earlier historians. The introduction to both volumes, however (to turn Panofsky's words against his own project), "betray rather than parade" their ideological agenda.[12]

In his introduction to the Dürer book, Panofsky declares that the German contribution to art history has yet to be acknowledged. He proposes that the artistic accomplishments of Dürer, whom he defines as a representative of the German national spirit, make him worthy of comparison with the great artists of the Italian Renaissance. While there is an interesting continuity to be traced in the nationalism of Wackenroder and Schlegel and that of Panofsky, the historiographic differences in the way they advance their claims are more significant than their similarities. The period of 150 years or so that separates the texts of these authors could be said to have witnessed the triumph of history writing. The historicist principle enunciated by Herder had been developed in the course of the nineteenth century into something resembling a science. The recognition that time decisively affects our understand-

11. Panofsky, *The Life and Art of Albrecht Dürer*, 2 vols. (Princeton: Princeton University Press, 1943) and *Early Netherlandish Painting*, 2 vols. (Cambridge: Harvard University Press, 1953).

12. The phrase is a quotation from Panofsky, "The History of Art as a Humanistic Discipline" (1940), in *Meaning and the Visual Arts* (Garden City, N.Y.: Doubleday & Co., 1955), 14. It occurs as part of the definition of what he called the "iconological" method of interpretation, the purpose of which was to uncover the cultural attitudes encoded in the "content" of the work of art.

ing of the world transformed all aspects of human knowledge; in addition, the influence of the success of the physical sciences during the same period pushed historical studies into an ever-increasing empiricism. The corresponding transformation in the function of history seems to depend above all else on the elimination of the subjectivity of the historian. Whereas Wackenroder and Schlegel willingly admitted that their interest in history grew from their religious and nationalist beliefs, in Panofsky's case, the historian's agenda is far less explicit.

The nationalism of the introduction to the Dürer book, for example, appears both paradoxical and curious in light of Panofsky's forced exile from Germany by the National Socialists. Inserting Dürer into the Renaissance canon of Italian artists was a much more complicated act than an assertion of pride in national identity. As I have argued elsewhere, Panofsky's view of Dürer as torn between the principles of reason and unreason—for which he used the emblem of Dürer's engraving, *Melencolia I*—has more to do with the political situation of Germany in his own time (that is, with a defense of humanism in the context of National Socialism) than it does with the cultural conditions of sixteenth-century Nuremberg.[13] Nevertheless, Panofsky's engagement with politics does not register as part of the conscious objectives of his historical biography. Political and emotional beliefs were repressed in favor of Kantian disinterest.

The same "objective" attitude is found in the introduction to *Early Netherlandish Painting*. Here Panofsky argues that Netherlandish naturalism, the characteristic quality of this school, is actually indebted to the invention of one-point perspective, the supreme artistic achievement of Italian art of the same period. The canonical status of Netherlandish art is thus buttressed by its incorporation of one of the pictorial devices that serves to distinguish Italian art. Instead of appealing to the notion of artistic relativity on which Wackenroder and Schlegel had based their claim for the interest of old German painting, Panofsky attempts to include Netherlandish art under the umbrella of traditional taste for

13. See "Panofsky's Melancolia" in my book, *The Practice of Theory: Poststructuralism, Cultural Politics, and Art History* (Ithaca: Cornell University Press, 1994), 65–78.

the Italian Renaissance. If Italian painting is part of the canon because it developed mimetic techniques (such as perspective) that enabled it to achieve more convincing kinds of illusionism, thereby heightening the naturalism for which it had been valued, then Netherlandish painting gains status by sharing these characteristics.[14] Similarly, Panofsky's analysis of the complex symbolism of Netherlandish painting, which is discussed at length, could be said to represent an attempt to find an equivalent for the complicated religious and secular allegories that are a feature of Italian art of this period. Once again, the artistic merit attached to early Netherlandish art would result neither from its pictorial autonomy nor from the principle of artistic relativity, but from its similarity to the southern European tradition.

What led to the suppression of the authorial agenda that seems to distinguish Panofsky's treatment of northern Renaissance art from those of Wackenroder and Schlegel? Why did the authorial voice become so much more removed and abstract? What occasioned the substitution of a colorless objectivity for a passionately argued subjectivity? A full answer to these questions would necessitate a history of the idea of history in the nineteenth and twentieth centuries and would explore the institutionalization of the discipline and the professionalization of its practitioners. It is immediately apparent, however, that history served a very different function for Wackenroder and Schlegel than it did for Panofsky. In the earlier case histories, the writing of history is clearly part of a larger cultural rhetoric; in its later incarnation, however, it seems to be pursued as if it could be an end in itself.

Panofsky's reticence about the larger cultural function of history, his reluctance to articulate the concerns that animate his scholarly work, and his conception of history as a positivistic discipline, find their theoretical justification in "The History of Art as a Humanistic Discipline"(1940). In this reflective essay, Panofsky suggests that the historian is involved in two very different types of activity. In responding to the work of art (which he defines as a "man-made object demanding to be experienced aesthetically"), the art historian must both "re-create" the work by attempting to intuit the artistic

14. I analyze the introduction to *Early Netherlandish Painting* in chapter 4.

"intentions" that went into its creation, and then submit it to archaeological investigation. The relation between "aesthetic re-creation" and "archaeological investigation" is an "organic" one.

> It is not true that the art historian first constitutes his object by means of re-creative synthesis and then begins his archaeological investigation—as though first buying a ticket and then boarding a train. In reality the two processes do not succeed each other, they interpenetrate; not only does the re-creative synthesis serve as a basis for the archaeological investigation, the archaeological investigation in turn serves as a basis for the re-creative process; both mutually qualify and rectify one another.[15]

The aesthetic re-creation of the work is deemed to depend "not only on the natural sensitivity and visual training of the spectator, but also on his cultural equipment."[16] Unlike a naive beholder, the art historian, Panofsky argues, is aware of his cultural predispositions; that is, he is aware of the contemporary perspective he brings to the work of interpretation as a consequence of belonging to a culture different from that under investigation. The point of the historian's recognition of his own cultural values, however, is neither to acknowledge them as part of the historical narrative that will result from his engagement with the past nor to understand that his response will inevitably be filtered through the peculiar configuration of his own subjectivity. Rather, the presence of these cultural values is acknowledged only so that they can be disregarded. It is by means of his knowledge of the past that the historian is to control, if not extirpate altogether, the affective and valuational attitudes he brought to the enterprise in the first place, becoming as "objective" as possible.

> He tries, therefore, to make adjustments by learning as much as he possibly can about the circumstances under which the objects of his studies were created. Not only will he collect and verify all the available information as to medium, condition, age, authorship, destination, etc., but he will also compare the work with others of its class,

15. Panofsky, "The History of Art and Humanistic Discipline," 16.
16. Ibid.

> and will examine such writings as reflect the aesthetic standards of its country and age, in order to achieve a more "objective" appraisal of its quality.
>
> . . . But when he does all this, his aesthetic perception as such will change accordingly, and will more and more adapt itself to the original "intention" of the works. Thus what the art historian, as opposed to the "naive" art lover, does, is not to erect a rational superstructure on an irrational foundation, but to develop his re-creative experiences so as to conform with the results of his archaeological research, while continually checking the results of his archaeological research against the evidence of his re-creative experiences.[17]

Because of the putative elimination of the subjectivity of the historian, Panofsky's approach to interpretation has no way of dealing with issues of artistic merit. This method could, for example, be applied to the interpretation of any work of art regardless of its quality or its effect on the scholar. What is missing is some way of articulating why certain works matter to the interpreter and others do not.

Panofsky was, of course, fully aware that the discipline could not exist without a means of privileging some works above others. His solution was to claim that the greatness of works of art was self-evident. Artistic achievement would disclose itself to the historian in the course of his empirical investigations:

> But when a "masterpiece" is compared and connected with as many "less important" works of art as turn out, in the course of the investigation, to be comparable and connectable with it, the originality of the invention, the superiority of its composition and technique, and whatever other features make it "great," will automatically become evident—not in spite but because of the fact that the whole group of materials has been subjected to one and the same method of analysis and interpretation.[18]

Panofsky's banishment of subjectivity in favor of positivistic objectivity—the sacrifice of cultural judgment in favor of a re-creation

17. Ibid., 17–18.
18. Ibid., 18 n. 13.

of the artistic intentions of the past, intentions that were to be validated by archaeological investigation—proved deeply influential. Contemporary art historiography has concerned itself primarily with the evaluation and criticism of his methodological concepts, "iconography" and "iconology," that have for so long dominated scholarly activity in our discipline.[19] The other side of the coin, the fact that this subtle and effective method of historical interpretation succeeded because it obliterated questions related to the personal experience of the historian, deserves to be recognized and explored.

Panofsky's bias against the insertion of the concerns of the present into narratives about the past would appear to be part of a historical tendency that is also manifest in literary studies. Barbara Herrnstein Smith has pointed out that mid-twentieth-century literary critics have also been more concerned with the development of theories of interpretation than with articulating the rationale that occasions their deployment.

> While professors of literature have sought to claim for their activities the rigor, objectivity, cognitive substantiality, and progress associated with science and the empirical disciplines, they have also attempted to remain faithful to the essentially conservative and didactic mission of humanistic studies: to honor and preserve the culture's traditionally esteemed objects—in this case, its canonized texts—and to illuminate and transmit the traditional cultural values presumably embodied in them.[20]

19. See Panofsky, "Iconography and Iconology: An Introduction to the Study of Renaissance Art," in *Meaning in the Visual Arts*, 26–54. For comment on and criticism of this method of interpretation, see Ekkehard Kaemmerling, ed., *Ikonographie und Ikonologie. Theorien, Entwicklung, Probleme* (Cologne: DuMont, 1979); Jacques Bonnet, ed., *Erwin Panofsky: Cahiers pour un temps* (Paris: Centre Georges Pompidou, 1983); Michael Podro, *The Critical Historians of Art* (New Haven: Yale University Press, 1982); Michael Ann Holly, *Panofsky and the Foundations of Art History* (Ithaca: Cornell University Press, 1984) and *Iconografia e Iconologia* (Milan: Jaca Books, 1992); Keith Moxey, "Panofsky's Concept of 'Iconology' and the Problem of Interpretation in the History of Art," *New Literary History* 17 (1985–86): 265–74; Silvia Ferretti, *Cassirer, Panofsky, and Warburg: Symbol, Art, and History*, trans. Richard Pierce (New Haven: Yale University Press, 1989); Georges Didi-Huberman, *Devant l'image* (Paris: Minuit, 1990); and Brendan Cassidy, ed., *Iconography at the Crossroads* (Princeton: Princeton University Press, 1993).

20. Barbara Herrnstein Smith, "The Exile of Evaluation," in *Contingencies of Value: Alternative Perspectives for Critical Theory* (Cambridge: Harvard University Press, 1988), 18. It is significant that the book Smith identifies as the most extreme

Panofsky relegated the question of artistic excellence to the realm of the self-evident, and effectively wove this evaluative judgment into the fabric of tradition. From this perspective, one can only tell what is self-evident by consulting what others have considered artistically exceptional in the past. It is alleged that by reading the past we can infer what is appropriate to the present, thus avoiding the necessity of projecting contemporary opinion into the process. The price of interpretive objectivity is the abdication of responsibility for finding in history a means of articulating the cultural dilemmas of the present. The principle of self-evidence is profoundly conservative; it is dedicated to the support of the status quo and ideally suited to the task of providing art history with "scientific" respectability.

Panofsky's equation of canonical value with traditional value was espoused and supported by Ernst Gombrich, arguably the *other* most influential art historian of this century. In his view, it is because art historians are the custodians of this tradition that they can be distinguished from social scientists, who approach works of art as if they were part of the material of culture. In a 1973 lecture entitled "Art History and the Social Sciences," Gombrich took it upon himself to defend art history's preoccupation with a canon of works that had been recognized as "great," critiquing those who advocated the study of works of art as cultural artifacts. He argued that whereas the study of historical circumstance would significantly affect our appreciation of the art of the past, it was no sub-

---

version of the anti-evaluationist stance, Northrop Frye's *Anatomy of Criticism*, was, like *Early Netherlandish Painting*, published in the 1950s. Smith's book is only one of numerous contributions to the debate over the canon in literary studies. For some other perspectives on the canon, see Robert von Hallberg, ed., "Canons," a special issue of *Critical Inquiry* 10 (1983), which included essays by Barbara Herrnstein Smith, Charles Altieri, Jerome McGann, John Guillory, Richard Ohmann, and others; Jane Tompkins, *Sensational Designs: The Cultural Work of American Fiction, 1790–1860* (New York: Oxford University Press, 1985); Robert Scholes, "Aiming a Canon at the Curriculum," *Salmagundi* 72 (1986): 101–17, and the responses by E. D. Hirsch, Marjorie Perloff, Elizabeth Fox-Genovese, and others in the same issue; Charles Altieri, *Canons and Consequences: Reflections on the Ethical Force of Imaginative Ideals* (Evanston, Ill.: Northwestern University Press, 1990); Jan Goran, *The Making of the Modern Canon: Genesis and Crisis of a Literary Idea* (Atlantic Highlands, N.J.: Athlone Press, 1991); Paul Lauter, *Canons in Contexts* (New York: Oxford University Press, 1991); Henry Louis Gates Jr., *Loose Canons: Notes on the Culture Wars* (New York: Oxford University Press, 1992); and John Guillory, *Cultural Capital: The Problem of Literary Canon Formation* (Chicago: University of Chicago Press, 1993).

stitute for the connoisseur's capacity to discern quality. For Gombrich, the canon

> offers points of reference, standards of excellence which we cannot level down without losing direction. Which particular peaks, or which individual achievements we select for this role may be a matter of choice, but we could not make such a choice if there really were no peaks but only shifting dunes. . . . the values of the canon are too deeply embedded in the totality of our civilization for them to be discussed in isolation. . . . Our attitude to the peaks of art can be conveyed through the way we speak about them, perhaps through our very reluctance to spoil the experience with too much talk. What we call civilization may be interpreted as a web of value judgements which are implicit rather than explicit.[21]

What was it that led leading art historians of the caliber of Panofsky and Gombrich to dismiss any discussion of the cultural qualities of canonical works of art on the basis that they were self-evident? What supported their belief that artistic merit was universally discernible? The unstated assumption underlying their position would appear to be a universalist theory of aesthetics.

According to the aesthetic theory formulated by Immanuel Kant in the late eighteenth century, certain works of art had the capacity to provoke a transhistorical recognition of their extraordinary quality.[22] The existence of the beautiful was thus something located in the human response to objects rather than in the objects themselves. By making the capacity to recognize artistic quality part of the definition of "human nature," Kant's theory offered a basis for the identification of canonical status with the judgment of tradition. Both Panofsky and Gombrich belong to the humanist tradition of which Kant's theory is a part. They share the conviction that human nature affords an adequate epistemological foundation on which to understand both the world and "man's" place within it. For this reason, they can assert that the artistic quality of certain cultural artifacts is self-evident.

21. Gombrich, *Art History and the Social Sciences: The Romanes Lecture for 1973* (Oxford: Clarendon Press, 1975), 54. Northrop Frye also suggested silence as the means by which a critic might validate the equation of the canon with tradition. See Smith, "The Exile of Evaluation," 24.

22. Kant, *Critique of Aesthetic Judgement*, trans. James Meredith (Oxford: Clarendon Press, 1952).

The humanist conception of human subjectivity as something stable, continuous, autonomous, and unmodulated by circumstances of time and place has itself been subject to devastating criticism in our own time. Psychoanalysis, for example, has tended to emphasize the contingency of human consciousness. According to Jacques Lacan, subjectivity is split by the acquisition of language into that which represents the desires and drives of a pre-conscious condition (the unconscious) and that which represents the codes and conventions that govern social life (the symbolic).[23] On this account, identity is shifting and unstable, constantly under revision as the relation between the unconscious and the social is renegotiated in the light of the everchanging circumstances of everyday life. Such a view of identity formation clearly militates against the concept of an inherent human nature, against the assumption that all human beings react to the same things in the same way, let alone works of art. The idea of a universal human response to art has been further undermined by cultural critics, such as the Marxist sociologist Pierre Bourdieu. In a materialist critique of Kant's aesthetic theory, he showed that in contemporary French society, the response to works of art differed widely according to social class: while certain social groups ascribed exceptional quality to certain cultural objects, others denied them any value whatsoever.[24] Anthropologists such as Johannes Fabian and literary critics such as Edward Said have drawn attention to the ideological agenda underlying humanist epistemologies, suggesting that the conception of the human subject as stable and unchanging, a self-conscious entity capable of knowing both the world and itself, is a dimension of the Eurocentrism that characterized Western culture during the colonial period of the late eighteenth and nineteenth centuries.[25] The age of empire saw a fusion of the desire for knowledge with the worldwide expansion of European power. The search for knowledge was backed by epistemological assumptions

23. Lacan, "The Mirror Stage as Formative of the Function of the 'I' as Revealed in Psychoanalytic Experience" and "The Agency of the Letter in the Unconscious, or Reason since Freud," in *Écrits: A Selection*, trans. Alan Sheridan (New York: Norton, 1977), 1–7 and 146–78.

24. Pierre Bourdieu, *Distinction: A Social Critique of the Judgement of Taste*, trans. Richard Nice (Cambridge: Harvard University Press, 1989).

25. Johannes Fabian, *Time and the Other: How Anthropology Makes Its Object* (New York: Columbia University Press, 1983); Edward Said, *Orientalism* (New York: Vintage Books, 1979) and *Culture and Imperialism* (New York: Knopf, 1993).

that precluded cultural differences; moreover, in every encounter with other peoples, Europe was chosen as the standard by which to judge the rest. The result was a subordination of other cultures to a European conception of civilization and a reduction of the different ways of understanding the world to what we know as "science."

In one way or another, all these critics suggest that the means by which individuals, classes, and cultures invest objects with social value are so varied that such processes cannot be considered to belong to the same category. If this is the case, then the concept of aesthetics, one intimately associated with the humanist conception of an unchanging human nature, is emptied of its content.[26] Rather than trying to reduce the rich variety of human responses to art to a single kind of experience, it seems more important to articulate the grounds on which these different responses attain the status of discursive practices.

Panofsky's attempts to naturalize the concept of artistic quality—or, to paraphrase Gombrich, the claim that quality is one of the implicit value judgments that make up our civilization—were never completely convincing. Among the most important (and curiously neglected) arguments recognizing the role of the present in the task of accounting for the past is Leo Steinberg's remarkably prescient 1969 essay, "Objectivity and the Shrinking Self." By insisting that subjectivity mattered, Steinberg rebelled against the antiseptic objectivity, the positivistic empiricism, of the art history of his day. According to him, the way in which the art historian's cultural outlook is modelled by the cultural circumstances of his own time determines the importance he ultimately ascribes to the work of art under consideration. Mannerist art, for example, had long been dismissed because of its negative assessment by the Italian art academies of the seventeenth century, but was rediscovered by twentieth-century Expressionist artists and critics on the basis of their own artistic preferences. In Steinberg's view, there is no evading personal involvement. All historical interpretation is necessarily colored by the beliefs of the interpreter.

> It is naive to imagine that you avoid the risk of projection merely by not interpreting. In desisting from interpretation, you do not cease

26. See Tony Bennett, "Really Useless Knowledge: A Political Critique of Aesthetics," *Literature and History* 13 (1987), 38–57.

to project. You merely project more unwittingly. There is apparently no escape from oneself and little safety in closing art history off against the contemporary imagination.[27]

It was not until the advent of feminism, however, that the equation of the art historical canon with tradition received a lasting challenge. More than any other historian or critic, it was Linda Nochlin in her famous piece, "Why Have There Been No Great Women Artists?" of 1971, who placed the issue of artistic merit squarely in the foreground of the discipline's attention.[28] She demonstrated just how unsatisfactory the concept of tradition was to a definition of the canonical status of a work of art by underscoring the extent to which a putative *master*piece serves to articulate and support a hierarchy of the sexes. There is nothing inherently natural about the selection of great artists and works on which art history depends, because that choice is the product of

27. Leo Steinberg, "Objectivity and the Shrinking Self," *Daedalus* 98 (summer 1969): 836. Svetlana Alpers also drew attention to the importance of the present in the interpretation of the past: see "Is Art History?" *Daedalus* 106 (1977): 1–13. Describing the work of T. J. Clark, Michael Fried, Leo Steinberg, and Michael Baxandall, she claimed that they emphasized the way in which the artistic merit discovered by past critics in works of art needs to be evaluated in the context of the present. In doing so, these authors implied that the canon inherited from tradition was not absolute and that it was subject to revision at the hands of succeeding generations.

Curiously enough, the social history of art inspired by the Marxist criticism of T. J. Clark has by and large taken the existence of a traditional canon for granted. Clark never conceived of the canon as a body of works imbued with historically contingent social meaning. While his own interpretations of canonical works are clearly politically motivated, he rarely calls attention to his own intellectual beliefs and social engagement in the process of his encounter with the past. See, for example, *Image of the People: Gustave Courbet and the 1848 Revolution* (Princeton: Princeton University Press, 1973) and *The Painting of Modern Life: Paris in the Art of Manet and His Followers* (Princeton: Princeton University Press, 1984). For criticism of Clark's failure to address the question of the canon, see Adrian Rifkin, "Marx's Clarkism," *Art History* 8 (1985): 488–95.

28. Linda Nochlin, "Why Have There Been No Great Women Artists?" *Art News* 69 (1971): 23–39, 67–69. See also Lisa Tickner, "Feminism, Art History and Sexual Difference," *Genders* (1988): 92–127, and Nanette Salomon, "The Art Historical Canon: Sins of Omission" in *(En)Gendering Knowledge: Feminists in Academe*, ed. Joan Hartman and Ellen Messer-Davidow (Knoxville: University of Tennessee Press, 1991), 222–36. Contributions since this chapter was written include "Rethinking the Canon," a collection of comments by Michael Camille, Zeynep Çelik, John Onians, Adrian Rifkin, and Christopher Steiner, in *Art Bulletin* 78 (1996): 198–217, and Griselda Pollock, *Differencing the Canon: Feminist Desire and the Writing of Art's Histories* (London: Routledge, 1999).

historically determined social attitudes. The equation of artistic merit with tradition, Nochlin argued, honored the cultural achievements of men because social forces prevented women from participating fully in the processes of artistic production. By means of a striking case study of the history of the exclusion of women from drawing or painting the nude in the art academies that dominated artistic education until the end of the nineteenth century, Nochlin suggested that social institutions, rather than an innate lack in female character, were responsible for the underrepresentation of this gender among the "great" artists of the past.

> Hopefully, by stressing the *institutional*—i.e., the public—rather than the *individual*, or private, pre-conditions for achievement or the lack of it in the arts, we have provided a paradigm for the investigation of other areas in the field. By examining in some detail a simple instance of deprivation or disadvantage—the unavailability of nude models to women art students—we have suggested that it was indeed *institutionally* made impossible for women to achieve artistic excellence, or success, on the same footing as men, *no matter what* the potency of their so-called talent, or genius.[29]

Rather than attempt to insert historical women into a social practice that had been constructed on the basis of their exclusion, subsequent feminist critics demanded the complete destruction of art history as a discipline. Griselda Pollock has used semiotics and the work of Foucault to argue that art history is itself a discursive practice, a way of making meaning that is imbued with the attitudes of the dominant gender. She concludes that feminist scholarship has no place within art history as it has traditionally been defined. Instead of addressing the canonical works around which disciplinary activity has revolved, she advocates what she calls "feminist interventions in the histories of art."[30]

Following Jacques Derrida, Adrian Rifkin has drawn out the consequences of linguistic theory for the art historical canon, focusing in particular on the necessity to recognize that the work of the historian—the historical text—is inevitably colored by the histo-

29. Nochlin, "Why No Great Women Artists," 69.

30. Griselda Pollock, "Feminist Interventions in the Histories of Art: An Introduction," in *Vision and Difference: Femininity, Feminism, and the Histories of Art* (London: Routledge, 1988), 1–17.

rian's position in history and culture. If art history can be regarded as a discursive practice, then it is susceptible to the type of textual analysis known as deconstruction.[31] Derrida has shown that language is involved in a game of absent presence, that it serves to bestow ontological status on what is otherwise only an unstable and shifting system of signs which draw their meaning not from their capacity to refer to objects in the world, but rather from the cultural attitudes with which they are invested by their users. In such circumstances, the notion of "art" is transformed: no longer referring to a series of cultural objects distinguished by its capacity to provoke a universal response to artistic merit, "art" becomes a series of cultural objects that has been arbitrarily awarded a privileged status by authors whose interests have been served by doing so.[32] The cultural category of "art" and the discursive practice of "art history" are social constructs, not constants in the history of civilization.

In the light of these critiques, we must rethink the function of authorial subjectivity in the writing of history, as well as the nature and status of the art historical canon. First, and perhaps most startling, we must realize that the type of appreciation expressed for northern Renaissance art in the work of Wackenroder and Schlegel is more relevant to the process of contemporary historical interpretation than is the work of Panofsky. Once the concept of tradition has been shown to be historically compromised, laden with the cultural attitudes of a particular historical moment, and once every attempt to make textual meaning has been shown to be less about the world than about the projection of authorial bias and prejudice—as well as insight and understanding—then it seems clear that art historians must address the question of why they believe the works they discuss are worth talking about. Once there is no longer anything self-evident about the status of the works that are the focus of art historical attention, it is necessary to explain why certain works have been chosen rather than others. The sub-

31. Adrian Rifkin, "Art's Histories," in *The New Art History*, ed. A. L. Rees and Frances Borzello (London: Camden Press, 1986), 157–63. See also Gerard Mermoz, "Rhetoric and Episteme: Writing about 'Art' in the Wake of Post-Structuralism," *Art History* 12 (1989): 497–509.

32. For a discussion of the way in which works of art are "framed," see Jacques Derrida, *The Truth in Painting*, trans. Geoff Bennington and Ian McLeod (Chicago: University of Chicago Press, 1987) and Paul Duro, ed., *The Rhetoric of the Frame: Essays on the Boundaries of the Artwork* (Cambridge: Cambridge University Press, 1996).

jective attitudes and cultural aspirations of the art historian become just as important an aspect of the narrative as the works that are its object. This is tantamount to saying that there is no canon beyond that which we ourselves construct. Instead of using history to buttress the existence of a traditional canon, instead of making the historical imagination serve the status quo, that is, the tastes of those whose culture we have inherited, a motivated history can be used to destabilize and call into question our culture's assumptions and prejudices by insisting on their contingency and relativity.

But these conclusions have profound pedagogical implications for art history. As a discipline organized around the study of a canon of artists and works guaranteed by tradition, art history was, at least until relatively recently, an agent in what Pierre Bourdieu has called the process of "cultural reproduction." The canonical content of our syllabi, for instance, serves as a means of transmitting "cultural capital" from one generation of the elite to another.[33] By transferring knowledge about a set of works whose merit can neither be questioned nor discussed, art history is often viewed as a conservative force in contemporary culture. How can this situation be transformed? The elimination of a canon seems to be a utopian dream. To suggest that art history could continue as a social institution without choosing which artists and works should be taught and which should not presupposes that the discipline could operate without a cultural agenda. Such manifest naiveté would simply reproduce the circumstances that promoted an unquestioning attitude toward the traditional canon in the first place. If we assume, in the wake of post-structuralism, that there are no disinterested narratives, that all art historical accounts are informed by one bias or another, then it seems wiser to acknowledge that there will always be some works considered to be of greater artistic merit than others. The standards that go into making such judgments change according to the attitudes and interests of different historical groups and individuals.

As I write, it is clear to me that transformations that accord with

33. Pierre Bourdieu and Jean-Claude Passeron, *Reproduction in Education, Society, and Culture*, trans. Richard Nice (London: Sage Publications, 1990). For an indictment of the way in which art history serves the process of cultural reproduction, see Carol Duncan, "Teaching the Rich," in *The Aesthetics of Power: Essays in Critical Art History* (New York: Cambridge University Press, 1993), 135–42.

these arguments are actually being carried out in practice. Rather than assume that the discipline might ever agree on what constitutes "quality," our students more and more frequently encounter concepts of artistic merit that respond to varied political and cultural beliefs. In such circumstances, they may be introduced to a formalist canon, Marxist canon, feminist canon, gay and lesbian canon, postcolonial canon, and so on. Alternatively, they may study the traditional set of works, but be given very different reasons for considering them extraordinary. This plethora of ideals of social value does not pretend to coexist in egalitarian conviviality. The value of acknowledging their struggle for attention is that none can henceforth be regarded as a "master narrative." Decisions to subscribe to one or another of their social agendas must be made with a full recognition of the political and cultural implications of that choice. In view of the alternatives, none of these initiatives can conceal the contingency of its assumptions behind the naturalizing mask of tradition.

Previously sanctioned narratives on which canonical status depended are being called into question by narratives that no longer share their assumptions. Individual artists and works of art—even entire periods—are being reevaluated in a way that places their continued representation in the canon in doubt, just as canonical status is now being sought for artists, works, and periods hitherto unrecognized. Indeed, as David Carrier has suggested, art history would appear to be experiencing a "paradigm shift." Using Thomas Kuhn's notion of the paradigm to refer to forms of art historical interpretation that are regarded as acceptable by the dominant institutions in the profession at any particular point in time, Carrier suggests that our discipline's notion of "truth" is being transformed and that we are witnessing the development of new paradigms of what might count as acceptable forms of interpretation.[34] Kuhn's sociology of knowledge not only affords us insight into contemporary circumstances but also presents a means of understanding change. Despite the appeal of some of art history's leading practitioners to an unchanging, constant notion of tradition, one that would stabilize and perpetuate a fixed concept of

34. David Carrier, "Erwin Panofsky, Leo Steinberg, David Carrier: The Problem of Objectivity in Art Historical Interpretation," *Journal of Aesthetics and Art Criticism* 47 (1989): 333–47. For Kuhn's theory of "paradigms," see *The Structure of Scientific Revolutions*, 2d ed. (Chicago: University of Chicago Press, 1970).

quality, the canon has always been malleable, seemingly engaged in a process of continual change.

This chapter, however, is not a descriptive account of art history's metamorphoses. Far from an empirical report, it is an appeal for a broader recognition of the role played by subjectivity in the articulation of historical interpretations. Rather than legitimate a pre-established canon of artists and works following the principle of objectivity, I argue that historians should pursue their own agendas and articulate their own motives for engaging in the process of finding cultural meaning in the art of the past. Rather than regard the subject of art history as fixed and unchanging, scholars have an opportunity to define what that subject might be. In doing so, they can display rather than conceal the cultural issues that preoccupy them. The subject of art history thus becomes manifestly an allegory of the historical circumstances that have shaped and empowered the subjectivity of the author.

This emphasis on the agency of the historian, his or her capacity to subject the values of the past to intense scrutiny and rigorous criticism, as well as to articulate the cultural aspirations of his or her own times, should not be misunderstood. This is not a call for some simpleminded correspondence between interpretation and interpreter, not a suggestion that one should reflect the other. The allegories of consciousness that we call "history" must inevitably be opaque. We can never be fully conscious of the motives that compel us to give one shape to an interpretation rather than another. The unconscious must, by definition, remain beyond our comprehension. Not only is the historian's subjectivity partly determined by unconscious forces, but it is also governed by the ideological traditions that are characteristic of its situation in history. Following Louis Althusser, we might define *ideology* as a social unconscious.[35] The historian's work belongs (sometimes knowingly and sometimes unknowingly) to a variety of ways of conceiving the relations between human beings as members of a particular culture, and of the means by which that culture relates to other cultures and to the world. These structures of understanding define his or her identity in relation to all other times and places.

35. L. Althusser, "Ideology and the Ideological State Apparatuses," in *Lenin and Philosophy and Other Essays*, trans. Ben Brewster (New York: Monthly Review Press, 1971), 126–86.

I conclude, therefore, with a paradox. The cultural codes and conventions that serve to define a particular identity also enable it to participate in social life. It is only because the subject is both constituted by and constituting of the circumstances in which he or she exists that the active role of history in the creation and transformation of culture can be understood. The call for a motivated history cannot assume that the historian's motives are transparently accessible. Psychological and ideological determination, however, cannot prevent an author from actively investing historical narratives with political persuasion that addresses the pressing cultural and social issues of the day.

CHAPTER FOUR

Perspective, Panofsky, and the Philosophy of History

For the things of the past are never viewed in their true perspective or receive their just value; but value and perception change with the individual or the nation that is looking back on its past.

—Friedrich Nietzsche, *The Use and Abuse of History*

The sign of history is henceforth not so much *the real* as *the intelligible*.

—Roland Barthes, "The Discourse of History"

Nearly five decades have passed since the publication of Erwin Panofsky's immensely influential study *Early Netherlandish Painting*—a work that effectively transformed scholarly thinking about this period and place of artistic production.[1] Not only did Panofsky alter our views about the significance of Netherlandish painting, but in doing so his book attracted dozens of scholars to the study of this art historical period. It is fair to say that half a century after the event we are still under the text's spell: it has played the role of a Kuhnian paradigm, dictating the kind of work done in this field down to the present day.[2]

How do we account for the long-lasting success of Panofsky's book, for the hold it still exerts over our imaginations? What theoretical strategies did he use to persuade us of the validity of his claims? What was Panofsky's conception of history, and how do we evaluate his historiographic perspective today? How does current thinking in the philosophy of history help us come to terms with the nature of his contribution, and how does it affect our own approach to issues of historical interpretation fifty years later?

It has always intrigued me that Panofsky should have opened his

1. Erwin Panofsky, *Early Netherlandish Painting*, 2 vols. (Cambridge: Harvard University Press, 1953).

2. Thomas Kuhn, *The Structure of Scientific Revolutions*, 2d ed. (Chicago: University of Chicago Press, 1970).

book on early Netherlandish painting, which was published in 1953, with a synopsis of his essay "Perspective as Symbolic Form," which appeared in 1925, nearly thirty years earlier.[3] A discussion of linear perspective may seem irrelevant to an artistic tradition that is not exactly identified with the geometric representation of space. Far from being an analysis of the particular illusionistic devices of Flemish painting, his is a lengthy account of the development and use of perspective throughout the history of European art. According to Panofsky, perspective is a conventional device for producing illusionistic space, the principles of which vary according to the historical moment in which they are elaborated. His teleological narrative recounts how the perspective techniques of antiquity were lost during the Middle Ages, only to be regained and perfected in the Renaissance. The Western tradition of perspectival representation is viewed as a kind of Hegelian dialectic, in which antithesis (the absence of illusionism in medieval art) follows thesis (the scenographic backgrounds of ancient painting) and culminates in synthesis (the one-point perspective of the Italian Renaissance, which allegedly combines the spatial infinity of medieval gold backgrounds with the specifically human qualities of vision). The moral of the story is that the system of geometric perspective developed in the Renaissance most closely coincided with later theories of space. As a consequence, Panofsky accords it a privileged place in the history of art; in fact, he uses it as the standard by which to evaluate perspective systems of other times and places. Assessing the naturalistic achievements of early Netherlandish painting, he claims that "the very weapons with which Jan Van Eyck and Roger van der Weyden were to achieve their victories had been forged in Sienna and Florence."[4] The basis on which Netherlandish painting is to be appreciated—the value that ensures it a place in the canon of great art, around which the history of art is constructed—is its incorporation or appropriation of the most effective means of representing space illusionistically, the perspective system worked out in Italy during the course of the fourteenth and fifteenth centuries.

3. Panofsky, *Early Netherlandish Painting*, 1:3–20. For his earlier work, see *Perspective as Symbolic Form*, trans. Christopher Wood (New York: Zone Books, 1991).

4. Panofsky, *Early Netherlandish Painting*, 1:9.

The introduction to *Early Netherlandish Painting* is both anomalous and ironic: it is as if opening a book on the art of the Quattrocento we should encounter an extended discussion of the descriptive qualities and the passion for detail characteristic of Netherlandish painting, and that these values should be proposed as the basis for our appreciation of Italian art. Svetlana Alpers has, of course, already drawn our attention to the Italocentric values that inform Panofsky's text, pointing out the ways in which they have severely distorted our understanding of Netherlandish art.[5] Instead of depending on the active organizing eye implied by geometric perspective, Alpers insists that Netherlandish painting depends on a passive eye, one on which the world is imprinted or recorded.

Rather than address the perceptual theories that lie at the heart of this familiar debate, I want instead to attend to the role played by perspective as a metaphor of knowledge. The issue, as I see it, is more a problem in the philosophy of history than a question about different systems of visual representation: I want to examine how a heuristic tool used for evaluating the achievement of Netherlandish naturalism itself became an epistemological guarantee for historical interpretation.[6] The irony involved in Panofsky's discussion of perspective in the opening pages of *Early Netherlandish Painting* lies in the omission of one of the most important aspects of his argument in "Perspective as Symbolic Form." The earlier essay has often been read as a conventionalist argument that relativized systems of perspective based on their failure to correspond with the physical processes of visual perception (as these had been determined by the perceptual scientists of Panofsky's own time). In the essay, Panofsky stressed the artificial and projective quality of perspective; his introduction to *Early Netherlandish Painting*, however, does just the opposite. What is highlighted instead is that Italian perspective corresponds with what he calls "modern" conceptions of space as continuous matter, even though by the twentieth century this Cartesian definition had been superseded first by New-

5. Svetlana Alpers, *The Art of Describing: Dutch Art in the Seventeenth Century* (Chicago: University of Chicago Press, 1983), esp. chap. 2.

6. For a comprehensive and insightful treatment of the multivalence of the perspective metaphor for Panofsky's work as a whole, see Brigitte Buettner, "Panofsky à l'ère de la reproduction mécanisée: une question de perspective," *Cahiers du Musée national d'art moderne* 53 (1995): 57–77.

tonian and then by Einsteinian physics. In other words, the geometric perspective of the Renaissance—viewed from the vantage point of 1953—is not just a device for obtaining illusionistic effects of space. According to Panofsky, it actually coincides with the way in which the world is structured.

The fact that Panofsky should have argued for the universal validity of Renaissance perspective in his introduction to *Early Netherlandish Painting* is not only ironic but also symptomatic of a deeper philosophical and cultural change in his way of thinking. The move from Hamburg to Princeton seems to have coincided with a profound transformation of his attitude toward history and method. Whereas Panofsky's early career was marked by a restless theoretical search in which he continually essayed fresh methodological experiments, his career in the United States was characterized by the attainment of certainty, a conviction that the methodological problems with which he had once grappled had been successfully resolved. The change undoubtedly had something to do with the tenor of thinking in the humanities at the time of his arrival.

During the 1950s, the disciplines of the humanities were overawed—and overshadowed—by the success of the physical sciences. An atmosphere of positivism dominated as the "human sciences" attempted to emulate the achievements of their empiricist counterparts. In addition, the United States experienced an unprecedented period of economic growth, which served to reinforce the spirit of national confidence stemming from the country's triumphant engagement in the Second World War. A twentieth-century version of the belief in the nation's manifest destiny emerged as the United States was called upon to play a role of world leadership. The challenge offered by the nation's only global competitor, the Soviet Union, meant that the American way of life, capitalist economics, and democratic electoral processes were rhetorically ennobled and broadcast as solutions to the dilemma of history. This atmosphere of positivist certainty and national purpose offered a fitting context for Panofsky's enduring concern to formulate a secure methodological underpinning for the discipline of art history. It may underlie not only his choice of Italian perspective as the accurate and "true" perspective but also its extension into a metaphor for knowledge itself.

There is, however, another dimension to Panofsky's choice of Renaissance perspective as an epistemological paradigm during his American years. Carl Landauer has argued that Panofsky's championing of Renaissance humanism, developed as a means of defending Enlightenment rationalism against the nationalist racist agendas of National Socialism, paralleled an American appreciation of European culture and learning.[7] Panofsky's promotion of the Renaissance corresponded with American admiration for that period as an emblem of civilization. Panofsky must thus have found in the humanist ideology of American higher education a welcome response to his erudition. American humanists, in their turn, would have approved of his invocation of Renaissance perspective as a metaphor for an epistemologically guaranteed form of historical interpretation.

What Panofsky underscores in the introduction to *Early Netherlandish Painting* is the conclusion to his earlier essay, namely, that perspective is a "symbolic form." The concept of symbolic form was elaborated by the neo-Kantian philosopher Ernst Cassirer, who lectured in Hamburg during the years of Panofsky's employment there. According to both Kant and his neo-Kantian disciple, human beings can never know the world: they can only make representations of it. In the absence of unmediated access, these representations—the so-called symbolic forms—acquire the status of knowledge. As Joseph Koerner puts it: "They are what make knowledge and experience possible in the first place, in a middle ground between self and world."[8] For Panofsky, the importance of Italian Renaissance perspective, the quality that makes it a symbolic form, lies in the fact that it is a system of projection that actually coincides with the way we see; it is the means through which objectivity and subjectivity become reconciled. Linear perspective both constitutes and structures our visual apprehension of the world.

7. See Carl Landauer, "Erwin Panofsky and the Renascence of the Renaissance," *Renaissance Quarterly* 47 (1994): 255–81, and my own essay, "Panofsky's Melancolia," in *The Practice of Theory: Postructuralism, Cultural Politics and Art History* (Ithaca: Cornell University Press, 1994), 65–78.

8. Joseph Koerner, "The Shock of the View," review of *Perspective as Symbolic Form*, by Erwin Panofsky, *New Republic*, 26 April 1993, 35. For useful discussions of Panofsky's use of the concept of "symbolic form," see Michael Ann Holly, *Panofsky and the Foundations of Art History* (Ithaca: Cornell University Press, 1984), chap. 5; Hubert Damisch, *The Origin of Perspective*, trans. John Goodman (Cambridge: MIT Press, 1994); and James Elkins, *The Poetics of Perspective* (Ithaca: Cornell University Press, 1993).

> Perspective, in transforming the *ousia* (reality) into the *phainomenon* (appearance), seems to reduce the divine to a mere subject matter for human consciousness; but for that reason, conversely, it expands human consciousness into a vessel for the divine.[9]

Perspective is thus a two-way street. It both shrinks the world to human proportions and provides humans with access to the secrets of nature. But for Panofsky, what appears to be a projective device, a system fabricated in an effort to make the world intelligible, actually matches the way in which reality is organized. Paradoxically enough, even though the perspective system of each period could be regarded as a symbolic form—that is, a means by which each period's characteristic process of making knowledge cannot be divorced from the knowledge it produces—Panofsky privileged what he regarded as the most advanced form of perspective, that produced in Italy during the Renaissance, as the one which was most suited to represent the methodological model on which history depends. As Stephen Melville has put it:

> The Renaissance achievement of rational perspective becomes the condition of the art historical discipline, and we are compelled to its terms whenever we look to establish another world view that would not, for example, privilege the Renaissance, because we can neither "look" nor imagine a "world view" without reinstalling at the heart of our project the terms only the Renaissance can expound for us.
>
> The way to Panofsky's understanding of the objectivity of art history lies through the Renaissance because the Renaissance provides the means to elide questions of the becoming historical of art; his valorization of perspective forges an apparently nonproblematic access of the rationalized space of the past. We are freed then to imagine ourselves henceforth as scientists of a certain kind, and within this imagination the grounds of privilege become invisible and profoundly naturalized.[10]

The discussion of Italian perspective in the introduction to *Early Netherlandish Painting* serves a double function. It exalts the achievements of Netherlandish painting by associating its naturalism with geometric perspective; much more important, it creates a

9. Panofsky, *Perspective as Symbolic Form*, 72.
10. Stephen Melville, "The Temptation of New Perspectives," *October* 52 (1990): 11–12.

metaphor for the role of the historian. History, like perspective, is not only a means of representing knowledge but a means of constituting (or becoming) knowledge. Just as the word *history* can refer either to what happened in the past, or to accounts that purport to tell us what happened in the past,[11] so the word *perspective* can suggest either one point of view among many, or *the* point which organizes and arranges all the others. Panofsky exploits the ambivalence inherent in the concepts of history and perspective, and suggests that historical interpretations do not stand for a past that is ultimately unknowable, but become fused with the past for which they allegedly account. Used metaphorically, perspective can suggest that our access to history is as direct and unmediated as our view through a window.

Panofsky's claim that Italian perspective coincides with the way we *experience* the world suggests that perspective affords us *access* to that world. His use of history and perspective is thus a means of naturalizing the process of interpretation, a way of suggesting that the historian's interpretation of the past is actually inscribed in the order of things. It is the power of the equation of vision and knowledge, enabled by the metaphor of perspective, that gives his book the rhetorical value of truth.

As historians aware of the insights of linguistic theory, we may contrast what I would call Panofsky's *perspectivalism*, his conviction that the interpreter's point of view creates and fashions knowledge backed by an epistemological guarantee, with Nietzsche's *perspectivism*.[12] According to Nietzsche, the metaphor of perspective relativized all claims to knowledge. Nietzsche does not view perspectives

11. For a brilliant analysis of the ontological function of the word *history*, see Roland Barthes, "The Discourse of History," in *The Rustle of Language*, trans. Richard Howard (Berkeley: University of California Press, 1989): "Historical discourse supposes, one might say, a double operation, one that is extremely complex. In the first phase (this description is, of course, only metaphorical), the referent is detached from the discourse, it becomes exterior to it, grounds it, is supposed to govern it. This is the phase of *res gestae*, and the discourse simply claims to be *historia rerum gestarum*: but in a second phase, it is the signified itself which is repulsed, merged in the referent; the referent enters into direct relation with the signifier, and the discourse, meant only to *express* the real, believes it elides the fundamental term of imaginary structures, which is the signified", (138).

12. See Alexander Nehamas, "Immanent and Transcendent Perspectivism in Nietzsche," *Nietzsche Studien* 12 (1983): 473–90; Nehamas, *Nietzsche: Life as Literature* (Cambridge: Harvard University Press, 1985) esp. chap. 2, "Untruth as a Condition of Life." See also Carlos Guillen, *Literature as System: Essays toward the Theory of Literary History* (Princeton: Princeton University Press, 1971), esp. chap. 8,

as different points of view on the same ultimately knowable reality; rather, he regards each one as incompatible with any other. Instead of relating to the same referent, perspectives are contained within their own discourse, and the reality to which they refer is unknowable.

> But I think we are today at least far from the ludicrous immodesty of decreeing from our own nook that there can only be legitimate perspectives from that nook. The world on the contrary has once more become "infinite" to us: insofar as we cannot dismiss the possibility that it *contains infinite interpretations.*[13]

Nietzsche's perspectivism coincides with—and helped form—an array of contemporary theories about language and the nature of human subjectivity, all of which have direct bearing on the philosophy of history. Like Nietzsche, many poststructuralist thinkers have been committed to erasing the distinction between objectivity and subjectivity. Instead of claiming, as did Panofsky, that the collapse of this distinction enables us to know the world, contemporary theory by and large has argued that its demise indicates that the world cannot be known. Language, for example, is viewed as a system of signs that, far from providing us with access to the world, bears only an arbitrary relation to its referents.[14] Others have claimed that the linguistic sign is not an abstract cipher in a system of rational communication, but rather one that is heavily freighted with the values of the particular circumstances in which is it used.[15]

"On the Concept and Metaphor of Perspective." For a history of the metaphor of perspective in the philosophy of history of the eighteenth and early nineteenth centuries, see Reinhart Kosellek, "Perspective and Temporality: A Contribution to the Historiographical Exposure of the Historical World," in *Futures Past: On the Semantics of Historical Time,* trans. Keith Tribe (Cambridge: MIT Press, 1985).

13. Friedrich Nietzsche, "The Joyful Wisdom," trans. Thomas Connor, in *The Complete Works of Friedrich Nietzsche,* ed. Oscar Levy (New York: Russell and Russell, 1964), 5:340–41.

14. Ferdinand de Saussure, *Course in General Linguistics,* ed. Charles Bally and Albert Sechehaye, trans. Roy Harris (La Salle, Ill.: Open Court, 1972); Charles Sanders Peirce, "Logic as Semiotic: The Theory of Signs," in *Semiotics: An Introductory Anthology,* ed. Robert Innis (Bloomington: Indiana University Press, 1985), 1–23.

15. Valentin Volosinov, *Marxism and the Philosophy of Language,* trans. Ladislav Matejka and I. R. Titunik (Cambridge: Harvard University Press, 1973); Mikhail Bakhtin, *The Dialogic Imagination: Four Essays,* ed. Michael Holquist, trans. Caryl Emerson and Michael Holquist (Austin: University of Texas Press, 1981).

Similarly, Freud's account of the formation of human subjectivity has been replaced by theories that argue that human beings are created as social subjects by means of their encounter with the signifying practices that constitute the culture of which they are a part.[16] By suggesting that the codes that make up our social experience are crucial to the formation of the individual, such theories argue that we are as much the product of culture as agents of its production. The consequence of these theoretical developments is that the use of vision as a metaphor for knowing has been widely discredited. Martin Jay, for example, has traced the history of the denigration of vision as a basis for knowledge in French philosophy of the twentieth century.[17] Similarly, in developing the concept of "situated knowledges," forms of knowledge that make limited rather than universal claims to validity, the feminist anthropologist Donna Haraway argues against a concept of knowledge based on the notion of the all-seeing eye in favor of one based on partial and partisan perspectives.[18]

At this point, it is important to make clear that this evaluation of Panofsky's philosophy of history in the context of contemporary ideas should not be construed as an attack, but rather seen as a tribute to his theoretical imagination. It almost goes without saying that my own critique is as susceptible to the same kind of analysis as that to which I have subjected his ideas. In other words, mine is not an exercise in ideology criticism, not an attempt to show how Panofsky's work represents a particular cultural bias from a position that purports to be value-free. It is, rather, a form of discourse analysis, an analysis of the unspoken values that inform his text from a perspective (not *the* perspective) that recognizes all points of view as necessarily ideological. There is nothing innocent in writing a text about a text. Whatever interest the conclusions may provoke can only result from the friction between the different perspectives those texts represent.

16. Jacques Lacan, "The Mirror Stage as Formative of the Function of the 'I' as Revealed in Psychoanalytic Experience," in *Écrits: A Selection*, trans. Alan Sheridan (New York: W. W. Norton and Co., 1977), 1–7; Lacan, "Of the Gaze as *Objet Petit a*," in *The Four Fundamental Concepts of Psycho-Analysis*, ed. Jacques-Alain Miller, trans. Alan Sheridan (New York: W. W. Norton and Co., 1981), 67–119.

17. Martin Jay, *Downcast Eyes: The Denigration of Vision in Twentieth-Century French Thought* (Berkeley: University of California Press, 1993).

18. Donna Haraway, "Situated Knowledges: The Science Question in Feminism and the Privilege of Partial Perspective," *Feminist Studies* 14 (1988): 575–99.

What are the implications of Panofsky's equation of geometric perspective with vision as a metaphor for historical knowledge, and how does this concept operate within the context of his book? One of the most dramatic demonstrations of the power of this idea may be found in Panofsky's discussion of the concept of "hidden symbolism." According to Panofsky, it was the ambition of early Netherlandish artists to offer us a complete illusion of reality. Iconographic analyses such as those by Charles de Tolnay, Meyer Schapiro, Millard Meiss, and Panofsky himself, however, suggested that Netherlandish painting also possessed an important symbolic dimension.[19] The problem for Panofsky was to reconcile an art that he claimed was wholly mimetic, one that had as its goal the imitation of nature, with one that was also symbolic. How could Netherlandish art be laden with theological significance without violating the naturalistic principles to which it was allegedly dedicated? The answer lies in the notion of hidden symbolism, which simultaneously implied both the presence of meaning (if the symbolism was recognized) and its absence (if it was not). The curious status of this long-lived heuristic tool derives from the fact that it is a logical impossibility. According to Panofsky, hidden symbolism is symbolic because it is naturalistic, and naturalistic because it is symbolic.

The significance of the metaphor of perspective as a device for the creation of meaning can be gauged by Panofsky's effort to sort out this creative contradiction.

> The application of perspective, we remember, implies that the painting surface is understood as a "window" through which we look out into a section of space. If taken seriously, this means no more nor less than that pictorial space is subject to the rules that govern empirical space, that there must be no obvious contradiction between what we do see in the picture and what we might see in reality. . . . A way had be found to reconcile the new naturalism with a

19. Erwin Panofsky, "Jan van Eyck's Arnolfini Portrait," *Burlington Magazine* 64 (1934): 117–27; Charles de Tolnay, *Le Maître de Flémalle et les frères van Eyck* (Brussels: Editions de la Connaissance, 1938); Meyer Schapiro, " 'Muscipula Diaboli': The Symbolism of the Mérode Altarpiece," *Art Bulletin* 27 (1945): 182–87; Millard Meiss, "Light as Form and Symbol in Some Fifteenth Century Paintings," *Art Bulletin* 27 (1945): 175–81.

> thousand years of Christian tradition; and this attempt resulted in what may be termed concealed or disguised symbolism as opposed to open or obvious symbolism.[20]

The consequence of the metaphoric use of perspective as a warrant for the work of the historian is that the "window on the world" translates into the capacity to see through the illusionistic surface of the painting into the hidden intentions of the painter who executed it. If the world of appearances coincides with the world of representation because a device for spatial representation coincides with a theory of vision, then the only means by which symbolism can be apprehended is by privileged intuition. As Panofsky is the first to admit, this perplexing conclusion places the interpreter in an awkward methodological quandary for which there is no solution.

> If every ordinary plant, architectural detail, implement, or piece of furniture could be conceived as a metaphor, so that all forms meant to convey a symbolic idea could appear as ordinary plants, architectural details, implements or pieces of furniture: how are we to decide where the general "metaphorical" transfiguration of nature ends and the actual, specific symbolism begins? . . . There is, I am afraid, no other answer to this problem than the use of historical methods tempered, if possible, by common sense.[21]

Panofsky's methodological difficulties are the direct consequence of his increasing dependence on a mimetic theory of representation. If Italian Renaissance perspective is, as Panofsky claims, congruent with the process of visual perception, and Netherlandish painting depends upon the Italian model, then the symbolism of Netherlandish painting must necessarily remain invisible. Critics of the concept of hidden symbolism, such as Lloyd Benjamin, Craig Harbison, and James Marrow, have rightly argued that if we conceive of Netherlandish art as conveying more than information about the way the world looks—that is, if we think that Netherlandish paintings are involved in manifesting and disseminating social and cultural values—then there is no need to consider the co-

20. Panofsky, *Early Netherlandish Painting,* 1:140–41.
21. Ibid., 1:142.

existence of naturalism and symbolism paradoxical.[22] There is in fact no theoretical necessity for a concept such as hidden symbolism, for if we replace the notion that mimesis is central to the work of artistic creation with the idea that as a form of social activity it is involved in the creation of cultural values, then there is no conflict involved in the location of symbols within the context of a naturalistic art. If the representation of nature is itself conventional or symbolic, something that Roland Barthes would have called a "reality effect," then the codes that suggest mimesis do not contradict those that refer to other aspects of cultural experience.[23] Once the entire fabric of the image is understood as a construction rather than something indebted to the duplication of visual experience, then it is possible to view mimesis as a code like any other. In these circumstances, all codes, whether mimetic or non-mimetic, are engaged in the communication of cultural attitudes.

The concept of hidden symbolism mars the coherence of Panofsky's account of early Netherlandish painting and underscores the theoretical limitations of his use of geometric perspective as a metaphor for epistemologically guaranteed forms of knowledge. Rather than rendering the events and images of the past universally accessible, perspective is perhaps more usefully regarded as a way of acknowledging that all interpreters write from a point of view. If we take that route, we can conclude that the interpretations advanced in Panofsky's book are not necessarily reconcilable with other attempts to discern meaning in early Netherlandish painting. But this conclusion need not invalidate his interpretations. Attention to the inevitable "perspectivism" of historical writing allows us to admit the importance of the present in our accounts of the past.

22. Lloyd Benjamin, "Disguised Symbolism Exposed and the History of Early Netherlandish Painting," *Studies in Iconography* 2 (1976): 11–24; James Marrow, "Symbol and Meaning in Northern European Art of the Late Middle Ages and the Early Renaissance," *Simiolus* 16 (1986): 150–69; Craig Harbison, review of *The Altar and the Altarpiece: Sacramental Themes in Early Netherlandish Painting*, by Barbara Lane, *Simiolus* 15 (1985): 221–25; Harbison, "Religious Imagination and Art-Historical Method: A Reply to Barbara Lane's 'Sacred versus Profane,'" *Simiolus* 19 (1989): 198–205. An imaginative interpretation of hidden symbolism (which argued that Panofsky's concept was a response to the concealed erotics of Annunciation scenes, such as the Merode Altarpiece) was presented by Hanneke Grootenboer at the 1998 College Art Association meetings in Toronto.

23. Roland Barthes, "The Reality Effect," in *French Literary Theory Today*, ed. Tzvetan Todorov, trans. R. Carter (Cambridge: Cambridge University Press, 1982), 11–17.

In fact, it is in history's perspectivism that its enduring motivation may be located. Once we abandon the quasi-scientific pretensions that once animated art history, we can appreciate the commitments that impel historians to undertake the never-ending struggle of making sense of the past.

CHAPTER FIVE

Nostalgia for the Real

The Troubled Relation of Art History to Visual Studies

When the real is no longer what it used to be, nostalgia assumes its full meaning.

—Jean Baudrillard, "The Precession of Simulacra"

One of the persistent features of art theoretical writing in the last twenty years has been the concern of a number of critics to insist on the "end of art," the "end of art history," and the "end of aesthetics." Motivated by a variety of critical perspectives, such theorists all address the grand narrative of "art" afforded by Hegelian philosophy. Some believe that we live at the end of the process Hegel described, according to which art should be viewed as the materialization of the spirit, the principle of enlightenment, as it makes its way through time.

Following Hegel, Arthur Danto, for example, argues that the age of art is over because the spirit has transcended its materialization in artistic production and has assumed wholly intellectual form as philosophy.[1] Although acknowledging that artistic creation continues unabated, Danto insists that the transhistorical drive toward self-consciousness is no longer realized in art. The teleological thrust of artistic modernism has come to an end: the narrative whereby the various modernist movements bore a dialectical relationship to one another, so that in contradicting its predecessor each new initiative sublated that which came before into its own nature, has reached its conclusion. The unveiling of Andy Warhol's *Brillo Box* in 1964 introduced a note of irony that rendered the process complete.

1. Arthur Danto, "The End of Art," in *The Philosophical Disenfranchisement of Art* (New York: Columbia University Press, 1986), 81–115; Danto, "Three Decades after the End of Art," in *After the End of Art: Contemporary Art and the Pale of History* (Princeton: Princeton University Press, 1997), 21–39.

> For the past century, art has been drawing toward a philosophical self-consciousness, and this has been tacitly understood to mean that artists must produce art that embodies the philosophical essence of art. We now can see that this was a wrong understanding, and with a clearer understanding comes the recognition that there is no further direction for the history of art to take. It can be anything artists and patrons want it to be.[2]

Other critics, such as Hans Belting, also follow Hegel in the conviction that art and art history have come to an end.[3] Just as artistic production has lost its internal necessity, so the principle of form, or style, on which a history of art could be distinguished from other forms of historical interpretation, no longer serves as a guarantee of the discipline's autonomy. The collapse of the idea of style as the unifying concern of the history of art has led to a proliferation of different histories of art, each pursuing its own agenda.

> The more the inner unity of the history of art understood as an autonomous discipline failed, the more it dispersed itself into the surrounding context of culture and society to which it was thought to belong. The struggle about method lost its sharpness, and interpreters replaced one compelling art history with several, indeed many, art histories, which, like methods, exist peacefully alongside each other like the different directions of contemporary art.[4]

For Douglas Crimp, the rise of the museum sealed the fate of art. Associating Hegel's notion of the "end of art" with the historical emergence of the museum, Crimp argues that art's institutionalization, its confinement in the museum under the aegis of an idealist theory of aesthetics, served to remove it from the context of

2. Danto, "Three Decades," 36.

3. Hans Belting, *The End of Art History*, trans. Christopher Wood (Chicago: University of Chicago Press, 1987); Belting, *Das Ende der Kunstgeschichte. Eine Revision nach Zehn Jahren* (Munich: Beck, 1994).

4. Belting, *Das Ende der Kunstgeschichte*, 22. "Je mehr die innere Einheit einer autonom verstandene Kunstgeschichte zerviel, umso mehr löste sie sich in das ganze Umfeld der Kultur und Gesellschaft auf, zu dem man sie rechnen sollte. Der Streit um die Methode verlor seine Schärfe, und die Interpreten ersetzten die eine, zwingende Kunstgeschichte durch mehrere, ja viele Kunstgeschichten, die als Methoden ähnlich Konflictlos nebeneinander existieren, wie es die zeitgenössischen Kunstrichtungen tun."

everyday life.[5] The idea of art's autonomy, its alleged universal value, is effectively responsible for its demise. While art continues to be produced, its autonomous status ensures that it cannot be an agent in everyday cultural and social interactions. The birth of the museum deprived art of its social significance, ensuring that it could only occupy a marginal position in the life of culture.

> Once materialized within the museum, idealist aesthetics could be expected to neutralize the possibility of art as revolutionary praxis or resistance. The effective removal of art from its direct engagement in social life, the creation of an "autonomous" realm for art, became the museum's mission, and it was against this that radical forms of modernist theory and practice were directed.[6]

Finally, in a context far removed from art theory, Western concepts of *art* and *history* have been challenged by a new awareness of the ways in which both are compromised by the existence of cultures which either have no cultural equivalents for them or whose potential equivalents for these ideas are so radically different as to be incommensurable. In his book *Time and the Other*, Johannes Fabian points out that in the context of colonialism, Western modernism's obsession with teleology and evolution effectively discredited and marginalized notions of time held by non-Western societies.[7] Post-colonial politics reminds us of the Eurocentric bias of modernist ideology. Modernist claims to universality can no longer be substantiated in an age that recognizes the value of cultural otherness. Just as modernist, or historicist, time once invalidated the time of other cultures, so our awareness of the legitimacy of different systems serves to undermine the Western project. In these circumstances, it is clear that there is nothing self-evident about the concepts of art, art history, or aesthetics. Far from belonging to the order of things, they have been exposed as cultural constructions that are bound to the times and places of their creation.

It is no coincidence that these various hypotheses should have

5. Douglas Crimp, *On the Museum's Ruins* (Cambridge: MIT Press, 1993).
6. Ibid., 303.
7. Johannes Fabian, *Time and the Other: How Anthropology Makes Its Object* (New York: Columbia University Press, 1983).

been advanced in the context of the philosophical challenge to the signifying power of language and to the master narratives on which the myth of modernism was based. The death of art, art history, and aesthetics can be viewed as a metaphor for the broader epistemological crisis inaugurated by deconstruction. In his essay "The Parergon," Derrida argued that in *The Critique of Judgement* Kant's attempt to distinguish art from other cultural artifacts on the basis of a posited universal human response depended upon the construction of aesthetic value rather than upon its discovery.[8] In distinguishing, say, a picture from its frame, ascribing aesthetic significance to one and not to the other, Derrida suggested that Kant discerned universal values in a culturally ordained distinction—one that was actually particular and local.

A failure to separate the study of art from the study of other kinds of images is often used as a criticism of the new field of academic inquiry known as "visual studies" or "visual culture." In this chapter, I shall attempt to argue that the animus directed against this new form of cultural analysis is misplaced. Rather than view the rise of the study of varied and often popular forms of image production—in which art is included in a spectrum of other kinds of visual products—as a potential threat to art as an institution, I would claim that the value of these visual juxtapositions lies in comparing and contrasting the study of each genre. The importance of comparing the study of painting, say, to that of television, or advertising, lies in understanding the different ways in which scholars and critics make meaning from each medium. The insights obtained by the heuristic strategies practiced in the study of one may well enrich the procedures used in the interpretation of another. While this view relativizes the study of art, suggesting that it is just one among many forms of visual production, it acknowledges the ethical and political concerns that motivate its students. The study of visual culture insists that there is nothing natural or universal about claims to aesthetic value, while the study of

8. See Jacques Derrida, *The Truth in Painting*, trans. Geoff Bennington and Ian McLeod (Chicago: University of Chicago Press, 1987), 37–147; also see David Rodowick, "Impure Mimesis, or the End of the Aesthetic," in *Deconstruction and the Spatial Arts: Art, Media, Architecture*, ed. Peter Brunette and David Wills (Cambridge: Cambridge University Press, 1994), 96–117.

art, as opposed to other kinds of images, can illuminate the particular significance attached to the idea of aesthetic value in different cultures at different moments in time.[9]

In viewing art from this perspective, in rendering it susceptible to comparison with other forms of visual imagery and the ways in which they have been understood, visual studies must openly acknowledge an agenda of its own. That agenda, I maintain, is inextricably linked to the philosophy of language. Basing itself on a recognition of the role of subjectivity in the pursuit of objectivity, a recognition that established fields of study are the record of an "archaeology" of discourse, visual studies is often concerned with the way in which objects reveal the ethical and political commitments of those who study them.

The term "visual culture" appears first to have been used by Michael Baxandall, and later by Svetlana Alpers, to refer to the spectrum of images characteristic of a particular culture at a particular time.[10] The introduction of the term was clearly motivated by Baxandall's concern, as a social historian, to incorporate the production of art into the rest of the social fabric in order to establish what he called the "period eye."[11] In doing so, he was not, of course, obliterating the notion of high art; instead, he suggested that the artistic production of pre-modern societies was not regarded as an autonomous activity but as one that was always vitally involved in the transactions that enabled and constituted everyday life. W. J. T. Mitchell, who is, perhaps, most responsible for the way in which the term is currently employed, envisions visual culture as a field of study, a focus for the interests of scholars working in many disciplines from varied points of view. As a member of a focus group at the University of Chicago, Mitchell helped develop both a rationale and a syllabus for a yearlong academic course in

9. The continued use of the term *art* in this essay, particularly in contrast to something called *non-art*, should be regarded as a way to refer to an ever-changing form of cultural discourse that deals with artifacts that are considered part of the heritage of nation-states, that play a role in the capitalist commodities market, and for which philosophical, religious, and/or political claims are advanced.

10. See Thomas DaCosta Kaufmann's response to the "Visual Culture Questionnaire," *October* 77 (1996): 45–48.

11. Michael Baxandall, *Painting and Experience in Fifteenth Century Italy* (Oxford: Oxford University Press, 1974).

the subject.[12] Regarding visual culture's relation to art history, Mitchell writes:

> From the standpoint of a general field of visual culture, art history can no longer rely on received notions of beauty or aesthetic significance to define its proper object of study. The realm of the vernacular and popular imagery clearly has to be reckoned with, and the notions of aesthetic hierarchy, of masterpieces and the genius of the artist have to be redescribed as historical constructions specific to various cultural place-times.[13]

If the distinction between art and visual artifact should be seen as a cultural construction rather than a cultural "given," then what kinds of imagery should visual culture address? On this point Mitchell is less specific:

> The point of a course in visual culture, in short, would be to provide students with a set of critical tools for the investigation of human visuality, not to transmit a specific body of information or values. If the questions and debates are posed frankly, as the very substance of the course rather than as something already settled, then information, values, and exposure to the finest productions of visual culture will inevitably follow.[14]

Such a definition appears to beg the question. The world of images is so vast as to necessitate a frame; having already dismissed "received notions of beauty or aesthetic significance," Mitchell's invocation of the idea of quality, his reference to "the finest productions of visual culture," as the grounds for determining the content of the course is difficult to understand. While his reluctance to suggest a frame for the study of visual culture might be regarded as providing a useful flexibility for a field that has yet to locate itself historically, that hesitation must also be regarded as a theoretical weakness.[15]

12. W. J. T. Mitchell, "What Is Visual Culture?" in *Meaning in the Visual Arts: Views from the Outside: A Centennial Commemoration of Erwin Panofsky (1892–1968)*, ed. Irving Lavin (Princeton: Institute for Advanced Study, 1995), 207–17.

13. Ibid., 209–210.

14. Ibid.

15. It is a weakness shared by certain other publications on the topic of visual culture which, in celebrating the heterogeneity of its potential subjects of study,

A more important drawback to Mitchell's proposed course is its ambition to provide students with "a set of critical tools for the investigation of human visuality." This sentiment, which echoes the goals of traditional art appreciation courses that aspire to enable students to "learn to look," suggests that there might be a simple set of concepts, a toolbox, with which the rich and complex world of visual experience might be understood.[16] If visual culture is not to be reduced to the study of art on the basis of a universal notion of aesthetic significance, why should its potential be foreclosed by assuming that there is a universal epistemological basis for the enterprise?

Rather than reduce the analysis of visual culture to a single set of principles, it seems to me that the point of the academic study of images is the recognition of their heterogeneity, the different circumstances of their production, and the variety of cultural and social functions they serve. It is precisely because the interpretive paraphernalia, the heuristic strategies, used in the elucidation of different traditions of visual production are so radically different from one another that each form of investigation has much to gain from a familiarity with the others. This, in fact, is the underlying logic behind the structure of at least one of the university programs that have adopted the "visual studies" title. In the graduate program instituted at the University of Rochester in the late 1980s, for instance, the curriculum in "Visual and Cultural Studies" consists of a variety of discipline-based requirements.[17] Students can take

---

fail to address the necessity to offer a focus, an agenda, or a rationale for the enterprise. See, for example, Chris Jenks, ed., *Visual Culture* (London: Routledge, 1995), which includes essays on topics as diverse as advertising, contemporary art, the visual experience of the city, fascist imagery, television, and so forth. Nicholas Mirzoeff's *An Introduction to Visual Culture* (London: Routledge, 1999) appeared too late to be taken into consideration in this chapter.

16. The formalist ideology of Joshua Taylor's famous *Learning to Look* (Chicago: University of Chicago Press, 1957) has been usefully contextualized by Linda Seidel and Katherine Taylor in their account of the social and cultural agendas that have determined the status and function of art at the institution for which Taylor's course was designed. See Linda Seidel and Katherine Taylor, *Looking to Learn: Visual Pedagogy at the University of Chicago* (Chicago: University of Chicago Press, 1998).

17. For a discussion of the aims of this project, see Scott Heller, "Visual Images Replace Text as Focal Point for Many Scholars," *Chronicle of Higher Education*, 19 July 1996, appendix 1. The program at Rochester has inspired a similar enterprise at the University of California, Irvine.

courses in art history, film, or popular culture, without sacrificing the specificity of the interpretive traditions associated with the individual protocols of each form of cultural discourse. Their exposure to disparate methodological traditions enables them to inform their own interpretations with an awareness of a broad range of viewpoints. In the study of art history, for example, they are capable of drawing upon theories and methods familiar to them from their study of, say, film or television.

More important, perhaps, an awareness of the ideological diversity implicit in various fields sensitizes students to the way in which the production of knowledge manifests the circumstances in which it takes place, as well as the interests of those involved, affording them insight into the changing nature of their own cultural activity. In being asked to familiarize themselves with the historiographic traditions that animate each discipline, students have an opportunity to analyze and deconstruct the philosophical attitudes and cultural values that have contributed to the frame constructed around those disciplines at different moments in time. A recognition of the shifting and unstable nature of disciplinary discourses, the ways in which they have responded to changing historical circumstances, enables analysts of those fields to evaluate the parameters within which they currently operate. The awareness that disciplines are not frozen in time—that there is nothing foundational about the methodological differences that distinguish one from another—empowers those who study visual culture to cross disciplinary boundaries with creative and productive results. If there is nothing sacred about the way in which a subject has been studied in the past, then there is nothing to prevent it from being viewed from another perspective in the future.

Needless to say, the rise of visual culture as a subject of academic interest has not gone unchallenged. Ironically enough, that challenge has come from scholars familiar with and sympathetic to poststructuralist thought as well as those dedicated to the preservation of the status quo. While the tendency to blur the distinction between art and non-art contains within it an implicit rejection of the idea of universal aesthetic value that has been the usual basis of art historical studies, it also seems to have offended critics long identified with new approaches to interpretation in the visual arts, including those who have explicitly rejected the idea of the humanist subject on which traditional claims for aesthetics are made.

In 1996, the journal *October* circulated a questionnaire to a number of academics who could be identified as broadly interested in the study of images, including art historians, students of film, and scholars of visuality in general, soliciting their views regarding the visual culture initiative. The questionnaire betrayed the suspicion of its framers: namely, that the establishment of this new field was an unfortunate development that catered to the exploitative interests of late capitalism. Since such a claim is clearly not self-evident, it is worth examining in some detail. Question 3 reads:

> It has been suggested that the precondition for visual studies as an interdisciplinary rubric is a newly wrought conception of the visual as disembodied *image*, re-created in the virtual spaces of sign-exchange and phantasmatic projection. Further, if this new paradigm of the image originally developed in the intersection between psychoanalytic and media discourses, it has now assumed a role independent of specific media. As a corollary the suggestion is that visual studies is helping, in its own modest, academic way, to produce subjects for the next stage of globalized capital.[18]

Who made this suggestion? Who said what to whom, when, and where, and what did that person mean by it? The disembodied voice of the text offers no clue, thus placing the potential respondent who seeks to react to these assertions at a disadvantage. What, for example, is meant by "the precondition for visual studies as an interdisciplinary rubric is a newly wrought conception of the visual as disembodied *image*"? If this is meant to suggest that visual studies seeks to separate the image from the rest of the cultural production that surrounds it, nothing could be further from the truth. The point of visual studies, as I see it, is to locate the image in the midst of the meaning-making processes that constitute its cultural environment. Such a definition implies, for instance, that visual studies deliberately ignores those guarantees traditionally sought

18. *October* 77 (1996), 25. For responses to the issues raised by this questionnaire, see Douglas Crimp, "Getting the Warhol We Deserve: Cultural Studies and Queer Studies," *Social Text* 59 (1999): 49–66, and Irit Rogoff, "Studying Visual Culture," in *The Visual Culture Reader*, ed. Nicholas Mirzoeff (London: Routledge, 1998), 14–26.

by scholars interested in preserving the autonomy of art. One of the assumptions underlying visual studies, I believe, is that the image is saturated with the word. While not denying the impossibility of adequately translating images into words, visual sign systems are inextricably bound up with linguistic and other codes that characterize a particular culture at a particular historical moment. As W. J. T. Mitchell puts it in his book:

> One polemical claim of *Picture Theory* is that the interaction of pictures and texts is constitutive of representation as such: all media are mixed media, and all representations are heterogeneous; there are no "purely" visual or verbal arts, though the impulse to purify media is one of the central utopian gestures of modernism.[19]

The assertion that the commitment of visual studies to a definition of the visual as a "disembodied image" is helping "to produce subjects for the next stage of globalized capital" is undoubtedly the claim for which the absence of support is most deeply felt. Rosalind Krauss's contribution to the same issue of *October* may clarify the argument, however. Her essay, entitled "Welcome to the Cultural Revolution," is a critique of the type of interdisciplinary work that has become known as cultural studies. She seems to suggest that in subscribing to a Lacanian theory of identity formation and an Althusserian theory of ideological interpellation, visual studies, like cultural studies, is in danger of succumbing to some reductive notion of identity construction.[20] She claims that this new field of investigation implies that human subjectivity is shaped by the passive reception of "disembodied images."

Such a conclusion seems hard to reconcile with the complexities of the Lacanian account of the formation of the subject. As Douglas Crimp has pointed out, there is nothing passive about the Lacanian theory.[21] If Lacan's description of the "mirror stage" suggests that the infant experiences a narcissistic identification with its own image, an image that is introjected to become an ego-ideal, that infant also becomes aware that its image is a mere object in the

19. W. J. T. Mitchell, *Picture Theory* (Chicago: University of Chicago Press, 1994), 5.

20. Rosalind Krauss, "Welcome to the Cultural Revolution," *October* 77 (1996): 85.

21. Crimp, "Getting the Warhol We Deserve," 53.

eyes of someone else. Not only does Lacan insist on the contradictory, or paradoxical, nature of the process by which an infant both identifies with and is alienated from an ego-ideal, but he regards this process as ongoing and never-ending. The Lacanian subject is thus never fixed but rather transitional and evolving. It is in the dynamism of this model, in the recurring construction and destruction of the ego-ideal, that certain interpreters, such as Kaja Silverman, have located the potential for individual initiative, the capacity of the subject to act as a social agent.[22] If the splitting of consciousness in the mirror stage depends as much upon the alienation of the individual from its image as it does upon the individual's identification with that image, then the creation of subjectivity cannot be viewed as a cause-and-effect relationship, and the connection between the study of images and the production of "subjects for the next stage of globalized capital" remains undemonstrated.

The rest of question 3—the argument that a poststructuralist approach to the study of the image, one that implies that aesthetic value is culturally constructed rather than foundational, is a manifestation of late capitalism—is hard to follow. Here the inspiration seems to be Fredric Jameson's influential examination of postmodernism.[23] Jameson subscribes to an evolutionary view of history, according to which postmodernism necessarily follows modernism because its culture reflects the nature of the late capitalist economy. While such an understanding views history as a teleological movement through time, in Jameson's case this is not a Hegelian model but a Marxist one. The engine of history is not the passage of the spirit; rather, it is the class struggle. According to Jameson, theoretical critiques of the grand narrative of Western history offered by Marxist thought should be regarded as symptoms of the historical moment in which they are formulated. Criticism of totalizing theories of history—in this case, the Marxist view—is thus considered a manifestation of the postmodern condition rather than a challenge to a traditional conception of history. On this

22. Kaja Silverman, "Fassbinder and Lacan: A Reconsideration of Gaze, Look and Image," in *Male Subjectivity at the Margins* (New York: Routledge, 1992), 125–56.

23. See Fredric Jameson, *Postmodernism, or, The Cultural Logic of Late Capitalism* (Durham: Duke University Press, 1991) and *The Cultural Turn: Selected Workings on the Postmodern* (London: Verso, 1998).

view, the Marxist understanding of history cannot be questioned because it is impossible to think outside it. History coincides with the real circumstances of human existence, and is not regarded as a particular philosophical outlook on those circumstances. Only if we accept a teleological view of history, one which identifies postmodernism and its intellectual developments as a necessary stage in either the evolution of the spirit or the evolution of capital, can the critique of historicist or Marxist philosophies of history be reduced to a characteristic of a historical period. Jameson's Marxism is necessarily a metaphilosophy, one which must encompass all other philosophical systems while at the same time refusing to recognize that it is one itself. It is this very lack of self-reflexivity, this naturalization of the grounds of historical thought, however, that visual studies seeks to challenge.

Based on a Derridean philosophy of language, one that insists that language is the home of metaphysics, visual studies focuses first and foremost on the frame within which meaning is produced. Just as discourse analysis approaches language as a code of arbitrary signs that are substitutes for the world rather than the route through which we gain access to it, so visual studies is interested in how images are cultural practices, the significance of which betrays the values of those who create, manipulate, and consume them. Rather than subscribe to a totalizing theory that reduces theoretical innovation to the ideological "superstructure" of a culture shaped by its economic "base," visual studies insists that despite the cultural forces that necessarily condition consciousness, human action is far from predictable: the very conflicts of cultural discourse (its heteroglossia) ensure that the principle of agency cannot be overlooked in cultural analysis. In the wake of poststructuralism—a set of theories that emphasized the indeterminacy of meaning and our inability to know the world—Jameson supports one of the more traditional of the grand narratives of history: Marx's claim to understand the relation of human beings to the real circumstances of their existence. In the context of a postructuralist philosophical tradition whose major insight is an acknowledgment of the opacity of language and its incapacity to provide access to the world, Jameson's theory of culture, and the attack on visual studies that depends upon it, can only be said to constitute a nostalgia for the real.

In his contribution to the same issue of *October*, Hal Foster joins Krauss in assuming a negative stance toward the idea of visual culture, arguing that this approach to images implies a move from "*art* to *visual* and from *history* to *culture*."[24] Taking the second set of binaries first, Foster claims that visual culture participates in what he calls an "ethnographic turn." In recognizing that positionality matters in the production of discourse, that knowledge is inflected by the interests of those responsible for its articulation, he claims that visual culture is in danger of compromising traditional (i.e., Marxist) conceptions of history.

> For in the ethnographic model one moves horizontally, from site to site across social space, more than vertically, in a discourse inscribed with a historicity, a responsibility of form, of its own. In this way the shift from history to culture may promote, in art as well as in criticism, a posthistorical reduction as often as a multihistorical complication.[25]

Foster thus opposes diachrony to synchrony, arguing that the latter gains at the expense of the former. A recognition of the spatiality of culture, of the multitude of subject positions that animate it, seems inimical to chronology. According to Foster, the differences between subject positions make it impossible to agree upon a single version of the historical events. Foster's misgivings are in fact misplaced. In dispensing with the grand narratives that have hitherto determined our conception of history, visual culture does not propose forgoing a philosophy of history. It is not time that is under attack by those who study visual culture, for it is precisely the interaction of the axes of time and space to which this field of investigation is dedicated. Abandoning the Hegelian and Marxist metanarratives allows us to rethink history from the perspective of cultural difference. Far from being a reductive development, such a move opens up the study of history so as to make its narratives potentially richer and more interesting. In other words, "multihistorical complication," the possibility of telling historical narratives

24. Hal Foster, "The Archive Without Museums," *October* 77 (1996): 104; see also his chapter "The Artist as Ethnographer," in *The Return of the Real* (Cambridge: MIT Press, 1996), 171–204.
25. Foster, "The Archive," 104–5.

from a variety of points of view, cannot be identified with "posthistorical reduction" without contradiction.

In replacing *art* with the term *visual,* Foster claims that visual culture surrenders the potential inherent in the concept of art's autonomy. Invoking "subjection" as autonomy's "other," he stresses that without autonomy, art is capable of being "reduced" to the merely visual. In an argument reminiscent of Adorno's view of art as a locus of resistance to capitalist culture, Foster writes:

> Enlightenment thinkers like Kant proclaimed autonomy in order to wrest institutions away from the *ancien régime,* art historians like Riegl to resist deterministic accounts of art, modernists from Manet to Judd to challenge the priority of iconographic texts, the necessity of illustrational meanings, the imperialism of the mass media, the overburdening of art with voluntaristic politics, and so on. Like essentialism, autonomy is a bad word, but it may not always be a bad strategy: call it *strategic autonomy.*[26]

It is no accident, of course, that the last words echo Gayatri Spivak's "strategic essentialism."[27] As in Spivak's conception of essentialism as either relative or absolute, depending on political circumstances, so the idea of "strategic autonomy" both relativizes and asserts the autonomy of art at the same time. In Foster's case, the assertion of the autonomy of art is a political gesture (one that is historically determined and subjectively freighted) meant to stave off the threat to art that is posed by the visual. For him, this is an either/or situation; either art is autonomous, or it disappears into the quagmire of the visual.

Contrary to Foster, I would argue that the binary oppositions of autonomy/subjection and art/visual are, in fact, inappropriate. The view that art is one of many discursive practices, a visual form of making meaning comparable in its procedures to other forms of imagery, means that these practices can be viewed as equivalent to one another. Rather than insist on the primacy of art in relation to other forms of cultural imagery, why not simply recognize its

26. Ibid., 118–19.

27. Gayatri Spivak, "Subaltern Studies: Deconstructing Historiography," in *In Other Worlds: Essays in Cultural Politics* (New York: Routledge, 1988), 197–221.

distinctiveness? Why not view art as one of the many kinds of imagery that constitute visual culture? It is not in the interest of visual culture to see art dissolved into other forms of imagery that surround it, but rather to acknowledge it as a distinct form of visual creativity, one possessing a historiographic tradition of its own. Indeed, visual culture should not only recognize the different genres of image production that animate a particular culture, but also insist that their unique qualities call for distinct approaches to their interpretations.

More important, perhaps, an approach to artistic production within the context of visual culture allows us to observe the social specificity as well as the historical malleability of claims to aesthetic value. Forms of visual production that have attained a certain status and appreciation within one culture need not attract this sort of attention in another. The Western concept of art enjoys global recognition and enables non-Western cultures to find types of artifacts equivalent to those prestigious in the European tradition, thus allowing them to compete in a political universe dominated by the idea of the nation-state. A recognition of the origins and function of this concept, however, reveals how the notion of art necessarily transforms the way in which the artifacts of non-Western cultures were once understood. Conceiving aesthetic value as a discursive practice also makes it possible for us to appreciate the ways in which the nature of such a practice changes in the course of time. A non-essentialist view of art, one that is not concerned with defending the "autonomy" of its enterprise against other forms of cultural discursivity, draws our attention to the changes in taste that serve to transform art into non-art and vice versa.

Visual culture has also been the target of criticism from Thomas Crow. Like Foster, Crow wants to defend the autonomy of art, but in this case the notion of autonomy is underwritten by an appeal to what he calls the "public sphere." Here, he follows Jürgen Habermas in arguing that the late eighteenth century saw the development of a bourgeois culture dedicated to the principles of nationalism that stood in opposition to the traditional autocratic authority of the state. It is in this public sphere, one allegedly characterized by an unfettered exchange of views through which public consensus might be forged, that Crow sees a guarantee for the autonomy of art.[28] The public sphere is the critical space in which an idea of what constitutes art might be discussed and consensus might be forged. Viewing the artistic situation in the United States in the wake of poststructuralism and the rise of identity politics, Crow laments the failure of an idea of consensual community, because it marks the passing of any agreement as to what constitutes artistic quality.[29] He ascribes the art world's lack of direction, the loss of an avant-garde, to the collapse of the public sphere, suggesting that special interests have sabotaged the communal basis on which the idea of art depended.

Crow's claim that identity politics has been responsible for degrading and destroying the public sphere—and thus compromising the autonomy of art—has been strenuously contested by feminist critics. Rosalyn Deutsche, for example, argues that the idea of the public sphere is in fact inimical to a democratic politics, particularly to a political scheme in which the interests of women might be recognized.[30] She points out that the unrestricted access and free exchange of ideas on which the concept of the public sphere depends are, in fact, utopian, and that the idea of consensus serves to stifle the interests of minorities rather than to engage them. Deutsche turns to post-Marxist authors such as Ernesto Laclau and Chantal Mouffe for corroboration, political theorists who would replace the notion of the public sphere with one of "radical democracy." According to this view, the open access, free communication, and consensus building associated with the concept of the public sphere give way to a recognition of incommensurable cultural interests and irreconcilable political differences.[31]

If, as I have been arguing, the notion of art is not necessarily opposed to the idea of visual culture, if it is possible to conceive of art as a particular circumscribed form of cultural discourse, one distin-

28. Thomas Crow, *Painters and Public Life in Eighteenth Century Paris* (New Haven: Yale University Press, 1985). His theory is based on that of Jürgen Habermas's in *The Structural Transformation of the Public Sphere: An Inquiry into a Category of Bourgeois Society*, trans. Thomas Burger with the assistance of Frederick Lawrence (Cambridge: MIT Press, 1988).

29. Crow, "These Collectors, They Talk About Baudrillard Now," in *Discussions in Contemporary Culture*, ed. Hal Foster (Seattle: Bay Press, 1987), 1–8.

30. Rosalyn Deutsche, "Agoraphobia," in *Evictions: Art and Spatial Politics* (Cambridge: MIT Press, 1996), 303–12.

31. Ernesto Laclau and Chantal Mouffe, *Hegemony and Socialist Strategy: Towards a Radical Democratic Politics* (London: Verso, 1985).

guished from (yet equivalent to) other forms of cultural production, how then might we define the breadth and scope of the imagery that the new kind of study might address? In attempting to answer this question, I do not want to be misunderstood. Any frame placed around the kinds of images that might be included in visual studies should be capable of redefinition and change. The juxtaposition of different traditions of image interpretation for the purpose of creating cultural meaning only makes sense if it allows for considerable experimentation. Visual studies should be flexible enough not only to permit but also to encourage and enable the imaginative comparison and contrast of hitherto unrelated forms of image production.

One quick way to reduce the new enterprise to absurdity, however, would be to suggest that it should be open to a consideration of *all* forms of cultural imagery, ranging from digital and electronic images to comic strips, without making qualitative distinctions between them. James Elkins has recently proposed that art history might usefully widen the parameters of its interests to include images that are considered non-art, such as graphs and tables that are used to convey information in the social and natural sciences.[32] He argues persuasively that the histories of the conventions used in informational imagery are little studied and that the sophistication characteristic of the study of art might inform the way in which these examples of non-art are received. If however, visual culture were to encompass all image-producing cultures, both past and present, its enterprise would be so vast and panoramic that its intellectual, cultural, and social agendas would be impossible to establish.

Instead of conceiving of visual culture as an expansion of the traditional activities of art history, in the way Elkins proposes, I would argue that the point of considering art along with non-art is not to meld the categories together but rather to maintain the distinctions between them. For only if we recognize the methodological differences among approaches to varied kinds of images can we realize the benefits of considering them in relation to one another. It is thus not a question of folding non-art into the study of art (just

32. James Elkins, "Art History and Images That Are Not Art," *Art Bulletin* 77 (1995): 553–71; see also Elkins's *The Domain of Images* (Ithaca: Cornell University Press, 1999).

as in the previous discussion of Foster's position, it was not a question of folding art into non-art), but rather of comparing and contrasting the heuristic tools used in making meaning from all types of image production.

The rationale for including or excluding different genres of image production from the category "visual culture" should depend on historical circumstances, educational needs, and political considerations. In our current situation, one of the most powerful reasons for including the study of art along with non-art lies in the recognition of the collapse of foundationalist theories of knowledge. Furthermore, visual studies opens doors to the production of knowledge from a variety of different subject positions. It fosters forms of interpretation inspired by feminism, queer studies, and postcolonialist thought. Rather than seek consensus, it benefits from radical disagreement among styles of interpretation. The heteroglossia that characterizes its operations is a positive and dynamic aspect of its activities. Indeed, the pursuit of differing styles of interpretation under the aegis of visual studies means that the particular interests associated with each form of knowledge production are hard to miss. Since it is no longer possible to suggest that knowledge is disinterested, the alterity of the juxtaposed voices will inevitably draw attention to the cultural agendas that inform the enterprise. Each form of argumentation can foreground rather than conceal its political affiliations.

A practical objection to the kind of interdisciplinary work envisioned by visual studies has been articulated by Rosalind Krauss.[33] She argues that interdisciplinarity threatens the skills traditionally associated with the discipline of art history. The capacity of art historians to distinguish the "hands" of different artists so as to attribute unknown works to known artists—in other words, their talent as connoisseurs—is threatened when they are faced with the need to absorb competing methodologies such as Foucauldian "archaeology" or semiotics. Art historians who participate in interdisciplinary programs, she argues, will take their skills with them, but will be unable to impart them to a new generation of students. The consequence of this process is that interdisciplinarity inevitably leads to "deskilling."

33. Rosalind Krauss, "Der Tod der Fachkenntnisse und Kunstfertigkeiten," *Texte zur Kunst* 5 (1995): 61–67.

I would argue, though, that this claim ignores historical change. Disciplines necessarily adapt to changing historical circumstances, and their theories and methods rise and fall according to their relevance for working professionals. Whereas for late-nineteenth- and early-twentieth-century art history, connoisseurship may have been an indispensable part of an art historian's training, problems of attribution no longer command the discipline's attention. The practice of connoisseurship has retired to the museum, where it is kept alive by the collecting impulses of civic and national pride, and to art dealerships, where its expertise is vital to the operations of the art market. As the concern to identify and date the objects of its study have receded in importance, problems of interpretation have risen to prominence. Quite apart from the issue of interdisciplinarity, it is not surprising that art historians should have wanted to move beyond the hermeneutic alternatives of stylistic analysis, iconography, and social history that were bequeathed to them by the discipline's founders.

The "deskilling" argument obscures the extent to which interdisciplinary work involves "reskilling," the acquisition of new skills to replace or add to old ones. Art historians may lose the capacity to distinguish "hands," but they may find intellectual strategies that are far more relevant to their professional practice today, not to mention their role as public intellectuals. Not only do recent theoretical and methodological perspectives enable them to carry out new and different kinds of scholarship, but in absorbing heuristic devices that are widely used in other fields in the humanities, they may make their work relevant to a wider audience. Such initiatives coincide with Jonathan Culler's vision of the university as a place in which knowledge is produced rather than reproduced from one generation to another.[34]

Finally, a word about the persistent strain of economism in Krauss's article. She draws an analogy between the deskilling of academics allegedly brought about by interdisciplinarity and the deskilling of manufacturing workers as a consequence of the rise of service industries.[35] The fate of both is said to play into the hands of a form of capitalist exploitation that seeks to make the labor

34. Jonathan Culler, "The Humanities Tomorrow," in *Framing the Sign: Criticism and Its Institutions* (Norman: University of Oklahoma Press, 1988), 41–56.

35. Krauss, "Der Tod der Fachkenntnisse," 64.

force more pliable by eroding the concept of "skilled" work. This scenario would imply that the narrative of the fate of academic skills in the context of interdisciplinarity is related to a more encompassing one concerning the operations of the capitalist economy. Far from attempting a justification of the social costs of capitalist strategies (a futile *and* unconscionable task), I would argue that the transformation of a manufacturing to a service economy involves as much a reskilling as a deskilling. Economic revolutions, of course, do not take place without pain and suffering. Is it fair, however, to equate the plight of laborers whose livelihood is threatened by the obsolescence of their skills with that of academics whose intellectual retooling might be considered a professional responsibility? Or is it possible that this reference to economic circumstances once again betrays a sort of nostalgia for the real, a desire—in the uncertainty of these poststructuralist days—to exceed the limitations of discourse in order to secure one's argument in the transcendental signified of a master narrative?

Returning, by way of conclusion, to the beginning of this chapter, I have argued that the rise of visual culture as a form of academic study coincides with the realization that we live in an age that has seen the end of art. The challenge to teleological views of history has been accompanied by a similar challenge to the transcendental status of the concept of art. Once the claims for art's autonomy—based either on the grounds of universal aesthetic appeal or on the argument that art provides a space of freedom within the context of capitalism—are recognized as politically inflected rhetorical strategies, strategies that are historically motivated, then it is possible to view art as one of many forms of cultural production. The paradox of this narrative might thus be found in its conviction that tradition matters, that we have inherited a rich and valuable discourse about art, while simultaneously asserting that this discourse does not have the transcendental status it has been accorded in the past. If this paradox is accepted, then we may readily place the study of art alongside the study of other visual practices, not in the interest of disregarding the differences that distinguish one from another, but in the interest of comparing and contrasting their theoretical assumptions and methodological procedures. Current theoretical attitudes toward knowledge production suggest that it is in difference rather than in sameness that the strongest contributions to the humanities are likely to be made. Each field of inquiry now has the opportunity to expand its repertoire of interpretive methodologies in relation to those around it. It is in the interstices between disciplines that the greatest insights regarding the structure of our knowledge, as well as our need to pursue it, are likely to be perceived.

CHAPTER SIX

After the Death of the "Death of the Author"

Autobiography reveals gaps, and not only gaps in time and space or between the individual and the social, but also a widening divergence between the manner and matter of its discourse. That is, autobiography reveals the impossibility of its own dream: what begins on the presumption of self-knowledge ends in the creation of a fiction that covers over the premises of its construction.

—Shari Benstock, "Authoring the Autobiographical"

But is the structure of autobiography different from that of fiction? The referent of fiction is forever absent; it cannot be called forth in its presence to give evidence for the truth of fictional writing. The fictional referent is "ideal"—produced and sustained by conventions and codes. But when is the referent, the object, of autobiographical writing present? When does he step forth to give evidence?

—Michael Ryan, "Self-Evidence"

The title of this chapter suggests a double negative. It implies that the poststructuralist "death of the author," the challenge to the authorial autonomy associated with the humanist view of the subject as something unified and constant, capable of understanding both world and self, is itself dated and possibly irrelevant. This, however, could not be further from what I have in mind. Far from asserting that two negatives add up to a positive, I would like to dwell on the paradox implied by neither/nor. Rather than suggest that the humanist subject should be resurrected, and that the production of knowledge should return to the universalist principles that legitimated it in the past, this chapter seeks to explore the conditions under which authorial identity might currently be envisioned. What are the epistemological circumstances in which art history currently operates? Did Roland Barthes's announcement of the "death of the author" eliminate the need for a concept of agency in historical interpretation, or has it instead forced us to reconceive the nature of agency itself?[1] If knowledge no longer depends upon the universalizing claims of the disembodied "voice from nowhere," how should we redefine authorial agency? Do the varied forms of identity that have laid claim to scholarly attention, such as those posited by feminism, queer studies, and postcolonialism, simply reproduce the universal pretensions once associated with the humanist tradition, or can the ideas of agency and identity be understood in terms that differ radically from those of the past?

Two crucial issues haunting the writing of history in the wake of poststructuralism are the question of identity and the definition of subjectivity.[2] Poststructuralist authors as various as Roland Barthes, Jacques Lacan, Michel Foucault, and Jacques Derrida argued, not so long ago, that the autonomous subject of the humanist tradition was a utopian dream of the European Enlightenment. This view of human identity had to be abandoned in a period that recognized the existence of an unconscious mind, the opacity of language, and the role of discursive practices in the dissemination of social power.

This revision of the idea of subjectivity has had important reverberations for our conception of knowledge generally and of history in particular. If identity is imagined as something unstable and changing rather than transcendental and constant, then human knowledge can no longer be viewed as a permanent edifice. We live in an age that challenges the very foundation on which that structure was erected. Doubts about the traditional premises on which the knowledge-producing activities of the humanities disciplines were once based have provided the justification for the introduction of a variety of politically inspired forms of interpretation, such as gender studies, ethnic studies, and cultural studies. These new approaches to historical interpretation no longer claim the epistemological status traditionally associated with positivistic scholarship. Their findings and conclusions are specifically defined as

1. Roland Barthes, "The Death of the Author," in *Image, Music, Text*, ed. and trans. Stephen Heath (New York: Hill and Wang, 1977), 142–48.

2. For reflections on the implications of poststructuralist theories of subjectivity for artistic production, see Griselda Pollock, "Art, Art School, Culture: Individualism after the Death of the Artist," in *The "Block" Reader in Visual Culture*, ed. Jon Bird, et al. (London: Routledge, 1996), 50–67, and Catherine Soussloff, "The Aura of Power and Mystery that Surrounds the Artist," in *Rückkehr des Authors?* ed. Fotis Jannidis (Tübingen: Max Niemeyer, 1999), 481–93.

forms of *local* knowledge that reject pretensions to universality. These perspectives subvert previously established knowledge claims by characterizing them as unavoidably tainted or colored by the values inherent in the circumstances of their production. The voice from nowhere, the objectivity posited by foundational epistemology, has come to be viewed as suspect because of its identification with Western culture, the dominance of white races, masculinist bias, and middle-class prejudice. The knowledge produced during the nineteenth and twentieth centuries on which the disciplines of the humanities were founded is now seen as one way of understanding the world, rather than *the* way in which the world can be understood.

This conception of the status and function of knowledge has had a dramatic impact on the history of art. If history is not regarded as *the* interpretation of the past produced from a neutral perspective, but rather as *an* interpretation of the past produced from a particular perspective, then it cannot be pursued for its own sake. The cultural function of historical interpretation can be openly acknowledged rather than masked behind an ideal of objectivity. As a consequence, the shape of the discipline has been decisively altered. Rather than operate according to an ideology of neutrality and disinterest that insists that the author repress his or her subjectivity in the pursuit of the facts—and rather than fetishize empirical data by suggesting that they might be relied upon to provide the interpretations that are actually forced on them by particular historians—scholars have begun to foreground their commitment to a specific form of understanding. In substituting an interpretive agenda for the allegedly impartial dedication to description, many art historians now offer us access to the methodological procedures and political goals that inform their views. What was once hidden in the interest of providing a common front, one that suggested that human subjectivity was universal in nature, now appears in the open, asserting the conflicting interests of different interpretive communities.

The consequences of these changes have been profound, if not always beneficial. Art history is now characterized by a cacaphony of voices, each seeking to represent the interests of different sectors of the discipline's population. Disciplinary conferences offer a variety of alternative points of view, all of which compete for the attention of the professionals in the field. In this situation, identity issues take on new meaning. It is not sufficient to destabilize humanist notions of the subject as essential and autonomous without reflecting upon the concept of identity that replaces them. The problem is effectively stated by Ernesto Laclau:

> Thus once objectivism disappeared as an "epistemological obstacle," it became possible to develop the full implications of the "death of the subject." At that point, the latter showed the secret poison that inhabited it, the possibility of a second death, "the death of the death of the subject," the reemergence of the subject as a result of its own death; the proliferation of concrete finitudes whose limitations are the source of their strength; the realization that there can be "subjects" because the gap that "the Subject" was supposed to bridge is actually unbridgeable.[3]

How is this subject (with a small *s*) to be theorized, if it is not simply to be an epigone of its ancestor? How is one, for example, to theorize the historian's relation to his or her text? Is there a correspondence between the historian's subjectivity on the one hand and the text on the other? Do the class, gender, or ethnic identities of the historian determine the nature of his or her intervention in the writing of history? How are the politics of identity inscribed in history writing?

In the course of writing this book, I have had to reflect upon my own relation to its argument. The circumstances in which this enterprise was undertaken are very different from those that reigned just a few years ago. When I wrote *The Practice of Theory* (1994), I assumed that the history of art still had a disciplinary center, and the voice I articulated was deliberately located in the margins.[4] I characterized myself as a historian interested in theoretical initiatives that had affected the structure of neighboring disciplines (such as literary studies, anthropology, and history), initiatives that seemed to have had little impact on art history. The point of steeping myself in these theories was to try to make them register in art historical interpretations, to use theory to destabilize the master narratives that had for so long dominated the discipline. I was

3. Ernesto Laclau, "Universalism, Particularism, and the Question of Identity," in *The Identity in Question*, ed. John Rajchman (New York: Routledge, 1995), 94.

4. Keith Moxey, *The Practice of Theory: Poststructuralism, Cultural Politics, and Art History* (Ithaca: Cornell University Press, 1994).

openly engaged in a polemic, championing change and transformation in the articulation of multiple discourses and perspectives.

In the years that have elapsed since then, art history has changed substantially. It is not as though the disciplinary establishment suddenly saw the light, abandoning a positivistic scholarship informed by notions of objectivity for one that recognized the impossibility of keeping subjectivity and objectivity apart. Instead, the establishment has accommodated itself to the new theoretical and political interests of many of its members. Indeed, there are relatively few institutions, with the exception of some university departments and an occasional fellowship-granting foundation, that have not responded in some way to the changes wrought in the discipline's way of doing business.

In an interesting twist of fate, scholars committed to established methodologies often characterize themselves as "pluralists." Under the aegis of "let many flowers bloom," these newly minted pluralists argue that since there is no objective way of determining the value of one interpretation over another, then all must be equally viable.[5] The apparent tolerance of this stance, however, masks the necessary tensions that characterize the relations between different forms of interpretation and often serves to defuse challenges levied against the status quo. It frequently fails to recognize that in the new theoretical landscape there is no such thing as a value-neutral position. Theory and method have become as much a part of the intellectual life of the discipline as empirical study. In these circumstances, pluralists have found it more attractive to legitimate their position and their power by appeals to tradition rather than by subjecting their own assumptions to critical scrutiny. Thus they deliberately evade one of the principal claims of the new perspectives, namely, that scholarly discourse cannot be disassociated from issues of power. "Tolerance," in other words, becomes one more defense against change.

Before attempting to characterize my own position, and locate my own voice within the new context of art history's multivocal discourse, I want to return to a consideration of theories of identity. How does a writer's personal consciousness register in a

5. For the function of an ideology of pluralism in blunting disciplinary change, see Ellen Rooney, *Seductive Reasoning: Pluralism as the Problematic of Contemporary Literary Theory* (Ithaca: Cornell University Press, 1989).

historical text? What is the relation between authorial identity and textual product? Theories of identity and the nature of human agency have been much discussed in the context of feminist theory. Following Foucault's suggestion that subjectivity is defined by the conventional systems responsible for making cultural meaning, systems he terms *discursive practices*, Judith Butler has argued that identity is both constituted by those practices and empowered by them to act upon the processes that gave them shape. Butler theorizes the instantiation of subjectivity by means of the concept of performance. Exploiting the ambivalence inherent in performance, she invokes its significance both as an act of repetition and as an act of personal agency. Identity (in Butler's case, gendered subjectivity) is a process with a prescribed script but a necessarily varied enactment. The performance of identity is a form of repetition without duplication, and it is this simultaneous production of sameness and difference, or difference within sameness, that allows for the conceptual possibility of agency.

> Paradoxically, the reconceptualization of identity as an *effect*, that is, as *produced* or *generated*, opens up possibilities of "agency" that are insidiously foreclosed by positions that take identity categories as foundational and fixed. For an identity to be an effect means that it is neither fatally determined nor fully artificial and arbitrary. . . . Construction is not opposed to agency; it is the necessary scene of agency, the very terms in which agency is articulated and becomes culturally intelligible.[6]

If, as Butler suggests, the subjectivity of the historian is both construct*ed* and construct*ing*—if subjectivity is an effect of discursive processes, and the link between an author and his or her text is relational rather than determined—then it is impossible to claim that the text is a reflection of a particular identity. Thus, the competing perspectives that currently characterize the history of art cannot be understood as wholly incommensurable with one another. Rather than fixed and permanent, the identities that manifest themselves in politically inspired forms of interpretation are themselves part of a process of change and transformation.

6. Judith Butler, *Gender Trouble: Feminism and the Subversion of Identity* (New York: Routledge, 1990), 147.

Joan Scott, however, has noted the persistence of the rhetoric of the humanist subject, of omniscience and finality, in forms of interpretation that respond to notions of identity in the production of situated knowledge. Such rhetoric, of course, could not be more opposed to the idea of subjectivity as process. Scott argues that the attempt to assert local interests by positing minority identities has often been subverted by a tendency to conceive of them in terms once used to ensure the dominance of the transcendental subject.

> The logic of individualism has structured the approach to multiculturalism in many ways. The call for tolerance is framed in terms of respect for individual characteristics and attitudes; group differences are conceived categorically and not relationally, as distinct entities rather than interconnected structures or systems created through repeated processes of the enunciation of difference.[7]

The temptation to view the contestatory subjectivities that have arisen in the wake of the demise of the humanist subject as radically incommensurable depends upon a survival of the notion of individualism associated with the *ancien régime*. This tendency, apparent in those whose political agendas have depended upon the assertion of differences *and* in those who have sought to discredit the politics of difference, is a travesty of the conception of subjectivity proposed by Butler. Scott writes:

> it makes more sense to teach our students and tell ourselves that identities are historically conferred, that this conferral is ambiguous (though it works precisely and necessarily by imposing a false clarity), that subjects are produced through multiple identifications, some of which become politically salient for a time in certain contexts, and that the project of history is not to reify identity but to understand its production as an ongoing process of differentiation, relentless in its repetition but also—and this seems to me the important political point—subject to redefinition, resistance, and change.[8]

Assuming then that identity is an "ongoing process of differentiation," what conclusions can we draw from the theoretical insights

7. Joan Scott, "Multiculturalism and the Politics of Identity," in *The Identity in Question*, ed. John Rajchman (New York: Routledge, 1995), 9.
8. Ibid., 11.

of Butler and Scott for the work of the historian? How do we conceive of the discursive practices of which the historian is an "effect," and what is the nature of the "agency" he or she possesses in the production of historical interpretation?

First of all, in order to intervene in the literary genre known as art history, the scholar must have acquired a high degree of general and professional education. Not only is the historian constituted by the discursive practices associated with educational institutions, but he or she must also absorb the reigning paradigms of knowledge production that characterize the historiographic moment.[9] The discursive practices of educational and professional formation are inevitably class-inflected. The art historian, for example, is necessarily implicated in the transmission of "cultural capital" from one generation to another.[10] A knowledge of the visual arts has traditionally been associated with the social elite, and, since the late eighteenth century, works of visual art have been identified with a form of spiritual value, known as aesthetic value, which has been an integral part of the cultural life of the bourgeoisie. The art historian is thus inextricably involved in both the creation and support of class distinctions. The art historical canon, that collection of works of art to which the history of art traditionally has dedicated its attention—a canon established on princely and aristocratic tastes, nationalized to become state property during the course of the eighteenth and nineteenth centuries—was both ennobled and democratized by means of the idea of aesthetic value so as to become an essential aspect of bourgeois education.

Does the art historian's formation by, and participation in, the processes by which class distinctions are perpetuated inevitably mean that elitist values are embedded in the histories they produce? Only the most reductive account of identity politics would argue that this is necessarily the case. If the scholar is both an effect of cultural formations and an agent of their construction, then his or her text may either transmit the class ideology of art history's academic discourse relatively unchanged, or it may bear only the

9. For a discussion of the concept of the paradigm in the sociology of knowledge, see Thomas Kuhn, *The Structure of Scientific Revolutions*, 2d ed. (Chicago: University of Chicago Press, 1970).

10. For a discussion of this concept, see Pierre Bourdieu, *Distinction: A Social Critique of the Judgement of Taste*, trans. Richard Nice (Cambridge: Harvard University Press, 1989).

most tangential relation to it. Given the importance of class identification for art historical discourse, however, I would argue that the historian's relation to the discipline's social function must always be significant. In evaluating the nature of a scholar's intervention in the historiography of the discipline, his or her understanding of art history's role in maintaining class distinctions should be of interest to any reading of an author's work. If the connection between the historian and text is relational rather than determined, as I have been arguing, then the inscription of class attitudes can take many forms. A fairly common one, for example, is the scholar who affirms the notion of aesthetic value, the idea that there is some spiritual sustenance to be drawn from works of art that sets them apart from the rest of the paraphernalia of everyday life, without recognizing that such an understanding of aesthetic value is a feature of a social elite with the cultural capital to appreciate it.

Second, quite apart from the ideological processes in which the historian is either wittingly or unwittingly involved, we must consider the unconscious or psychoanalytic mechanisms that characterize the historian's work both as a scholar of the past and as a pedagogue of future generations. In other words, how rationally are disciplinary paradigms of knowledge production transmitted and received? To what extent is the absorption of the discursive practices to which art history's methodological alternatives belong unconsciously determined rather than consciously chosen?

Dominick LaCapra has pointed out that the situation in which a graduate student acquires the interpretive models of a discipline, that is, his or her relation to a professor, is analogous to the relation that exists between an analyst and an analysand in psychoanalysis.[11] The student is bound to the historiography of the discipline in a highly personal manner, one in which an unconscious bond may well be as important as a conscious one. Just as the analysand adopts certain attitudes of the analyst in the attempt to restructure past experience in relation to the present, a process known as transference, so the student will adopt some of the characteristics of the professor in order to transform him-or herself into a figure of equivalent cultural authority. This kind of identification often results in the perpetuation of accepted forms of mean-

11. Dominick LaCapra, "History and Psychoanalysis," in *Soundings in Critical Theory* (Ithaca: Cornell University Press, 1989), 30–66.

ing production at the expense of more innovative alternatives. Even if the student consciously repudiates the models absorbed during the training period, that rejection will itself be relevant to critical evaluation of his or her eventual historiographic contribution. The rejection might, for example, represent an "anxiety of influence," a fear of imitating a respected authority and a desire to break out of a professional mold in order to claim an authority equivalent or superior to that of the original mentor.[12]

And third, the discursive practices of professional formation demand that the art historian put a personal stamp on literary production, regardless of whether the scholar is simply duplicating or creatively extending and manipulating an established disciplinary paradigm. Paradoxical as it appears in a positivist tradition that insists that the historian's task is to afford the public access to the truth—a process that might be undertaken, presumably, by anyone with the time, training, and inclination to do so—the conventions of professional life insist that each scholar distinguish his or her contribution from those of peers. It is one of the ironies of positivism that it should have emphasized rather than erased the role of the individual interpreter. The call for the construction of a unique subjectivity, the cult of the exceptional individual, is, of course, the heritage of a culture deeply invested in the ideology of the humanist subject. The degree to which a historian is susceptible to these ideological demands will also register significantly in any account of the discipline's history.[13]

I hope that this sketch of some of the discursive practices that constitute, enable, and empower historical writing might help us to think about the relation of historian and interpretive text. Because the drives and neuroses that determine the historian's psychological formation and the nature of the discursive practices that shape his or her professional identity are not necessarily open to self-reflection, it is inevitable that the character of the individual historical narrative, its full implications for the historical moment in which it is composed, can never be fully recognized. (Often, the process of

12. Harold Bloom, *The Anxiety of Influence: A Theory of Poetry* (New York: Oxford University Press, 1973).

13. The ideology of individualism is also the precondition for autobiography as a literary genre. See Georges Gunsdorf, "Conditions and Limits of Autobiography," trans. James Olney, in *Autobiography: Essays Theoretical and Critical*, ed. James Olney (Princeton: Princeton University Press, 1980), 28–48.

research and writing must come to an end before the scholar can perceive the pattern that informs the work.) As LaCapra points out, in the case of the historian there may well be a psychological mechanism that serves to make the work opaque to its creator.

In light of this, it is possible to argue both that a historical text bears only an oblique relationship to authorial identity—that is, the relation is mediated by a variety of cultural and psychological considerations—*and* that the text is nothing but an extended metaphor for the author's psychological, cultural, and professional formation, as well as for his or her participation in the pre-established discursive practices which enable the creation of historical meaning. If, on the one hand, the full significance of a historical text is never available to its author, and if, on the other, it is impossible for the historian to discern the past because access is mediated by the historically determined and psychologically inflected paradigms of meaning production that frame that encounter, then it seems possible to conclude that there is no relation between a historical text and its author *and*, simultaneously, that the text is an allegory of authorial identity. It is precisely the lack of a one-to-one correspondence between the discursive practices that have shaped the historian and the texts he or she produces that makes an analysis of the historian's life *and* an analysis of the historical text relevant to an assessment of that text's historiographic significance. While Barthes was correct in insisting that the passage from author to text is barred by the angel with the flaming sword, this does not necessarily mean that both life *and* text, signs belonging to different registers or codes, cannot be of value to those seeking to make sense of the past.

Given the complexity of the author/text relation, it seems paradoxical to reintroduce a reference to this book's manifest role in contemporary debates about the nature of art history as a discipline. Some of the chapters constitute a plea for greater theoretical and methodological diversity in the discipline's interpretive procedures, while others seek to articulate the ways in which the discursive practices that constitute the discipline's intellectual history reveal the attitudes that characterize their cultural location, as well as the way in which particular historians have either reiterated those ideologies or called them into question in the process of constructing their own interventions. My purpose in theorizing the role of identity and subjectivity in the production of historical narratives is to denaturalize disciplinary traditions that seek to maintain the idea that the historical voice is at best always a disembodied voice.

In calling attention to my own investment in these metahistorical narratives, I am keenly aware of the debate that swirls around the role of autobiography in scholarly writing.[14] The introduction of the personal into a discursive practice such as historical writing can often constitute a form of essentialism, a way to posit a direct connection between an author and his or her text. In this scenario, the autobiographical serves to ground the narrative in the author's experience in such a way as to make the intimate bond between subjectivity and memory serve as an unassailable foundation for the views being presented. By this logic, for example, only African Americans can represent the views of African Americans, and only women can articulate feminist agendas.

The concept of experience, that allegedly unmediated foundation on which claims to situated knowledge are sometimes based, has been usefully theorized by Joan Scott whose discussion of identity I referred to earlier. Arguing that there is nothing transparent or immediate about appeals to biography, she suggests that those events we consider crucial to our definition of self are always decided in retrospect. Indeed, the Freudian concept of *Nachträglichkeit* suggests that what our memories call experience is subject to a continual process of change, as those memories are recalled in the dynamic circumstances of the present.[15] The quotidian flow of events makes no distinction between those experiences we deem formative and those we do not; indeed, only in retrospect does the process of transforming an event into an experience reveal the thought involved in that metamorphosis. And some of the most important events that have affected us, those of a traumatic nature, cannot be recalled in their original form, but only through the filter of constructed memories.

> It is not individuals who have experience, but subjects who are constituted through experience. Experience in this definition then be-

14. See Gertrude Himmelfarb, "Professor Narcissus: In Today's Academy, Everything is Personal," *The Weekly Standard*, 2 June 1997, 17–21.

15. J. Laplanche and J. B. Pontalis, *The Language of Psychoanalysis*, trans. Donald Nicholson-Smith (New York: Norton, 1973), 111–14.

comes not the origin of our explanation, not the authoritative (because seen or felt) evidence that grounds what is known, but rather that which we seek to explain, that about which knowledge is produced. To think about experience in this way is to historicize it as well as to historicize the identities it produces.[16]

If, as I have been arguing, there is no direct correspondence between an author and his or her text, then what is the point of introducing the so-called personal at all? What epistemological purpose can reference to biography serve in understanding a text, if it is impossible to demonstrate the connection between them? Returning to Butler's notion of performance allows us to conceive of a particular subjectivity's acts of agency as both (1) *prescribed*, in the sense of having been installed in that subjectivity by means of the discursive practices that brought it into being, and (2) *instantiated*, as those discursive practices must be enacted by the subjectivity in question in everchanging circumstances that necessarily endow them with new meaning. Just as it is necessary for an appreciation of a scholar's historiographic location to acknowledge the psychological and cultural processes by which he or she was formed, so it is appropriate to consider the autobiographical account of the author responsible for the production of a specific text.

The function of autobiography has been extensively theorized in the wake of Roland Barthes's remarkable autobiographical sketch, *Roland Barthes par Roland Barthes*. Barthes insists on textualizing his life, rigorously refusing to see through the web of language to some underlying reality, arguing that our notions of subjectivity are the product of language itself.

> This book consists of what I do not know: the unconscious and ideology, things which utter themselves only by the voices of others. I cannot put on stage (in the text), *as such*, the symbolic and the ideological which pass through me, since I am their blind spot. . . .[17]

16. Scott, "The Evidence of Experience," *Critical Inquiry* 17 (1991): 779–80. For an earlier articulation of a similar point of view, see Teresa de Lauretis, "Semiotics and Experience," in *Alice Doesn't: Feminism, Semiotics, Cinema* (Bloomington: Indiana University Press, 1984), 158–86.

17. Roland Barthes, *Roland Barthes par Roland Barthes*, trans. Richard Howard (New York: Hill and Wang, 1977), 152.

Barthes's view foreshadows the more radical position of Derrida, for whom language alienates subjectivity from experience. His insistence that the "truth" of language lies in what is invested in it by those who use it, rather than in its relation to the world, means that autobiographical narratives represent only the order that their authors have imposed on their existential circumstances, not those circumstances themselves.[18] Derrida's follower Paul de Man claims that language even denies subjectivity the capacity to inflect and manipulate the processes by which meaning is made, implying that language inflicts a kind of metaphorical death on the notion of the subject as agent.[19]

The idea that the subject is the product of language rather than its creator, however, has been interpreted very differently by other theorists of autobiography. James Olney and Paul John Eakin, as well as Liz Stanley, Shari Benstock, and other feminist authors, interpret the prescriptive power of language positively, regarding it as an empowering process that, in Butler's terms, enables particular subjectivities to play a performative and therefore an active role within the culture that shapes them.[20] For Olney, autobiography is not a reference to some pre-established reality but rather a metaphor for the subject's attempt to make order of the universe.

> A metaphor, then, through which we stamp our own image on the face of nature, allows us to connect the known of ourselves to the unknown of the world, and, making available new relational patterns it simultaneously organizes the self into a new and richer entity; so

18. Robert Smith, *Derrida and Autobiography* (Cambridge: Cambridge University Press, 1995).

19. Paul de Man, "Autobiography as De-facement," *Modern Language Notes* 94 (1979): 919–30.

20. See James Olney, *Metaphors of the Self: The Meaning of Autobiography* (Princeton: Princeton University Press, 1972); Paul John Eakin, *Fictions in Autobiography: Studies in the Art of Self-Invention* (Princeton: Princeton University Press, 1985); Shari Benstock, ed., *The Private Self: Theory and Practice of Women's Autobiographical Writings* (Chapel Hill: University of North Carolina Press, 1988); Bella Brodzki and Celeste Schenck, eds., *Life/Lines: Theorizing Women's Autobiography* (Ithaca: Cornell University Press, 1988); Liz Stanley, *The Auto/Biographical I: The Theory and Practice of Feminist Auto-Biography* (Manchester: Manchester University Press, 1992); Kathleen Ashley, Leigh Gilmore, and Gerald Peters, eds., *Autobiography and Postmodernism* (Amherst: University of Massachusetts Press, 1994); and Leigh Gilmore, *Autobiographics: A Feminist Theory of Women's Self-Representation* (Ithaca: Cornell University Press, 1994). I am grateful to Janet Wolff for some of these references.

> that the old known self is joined to and transformed into the new and heretofore unknown self.[21]

Pursuing this line of thought, Nancy Miller argues that autobiography is a "self-fiction," yet one that enables the historiographer to comprehend the purposes behind the author's writing. She maintains that the introduction of the personal into the discursive practice of writing is not necessarily a form of essentialism, not a way of suggesting that there is a correspondence between author and text, for autobiography must necessarily be a carefully edited version of personal experience that depends for its shape on the deferred action of memory. Autobiography tells us which events in the author's life have been dignified with the status of experiences, which of those experiences the author identifies with, and which he or she does not. The insertion of an autobiographical myth is thought by Miller to be a form of "personal materialism," one that calls attention to who is speaking.

> By the risks of its writing, personal criticism embodies a pact, like the "autobiographical pact" binding writer to reader in the fabrication of self-truth, that what is at stake matters also to others: somewhere in the self-fiction of the personal voice is a belief that the writing is worth the risk. In this sense, by turning its authorial voice into spectacle, personal writing theorizes the stakes of its own performance: a personal materialism.[22]

The value of Miller's conception of the personal as autobiographical myth rather than autobiographical fact allows us to consider the crucial function of the anecdote in a new light. Joel Fineman, for example, has theorized the anecdote as the creation of a "reality effect," a way in which say, a historian, can nest one narrative within another so that they mutually reinforce each other's claims to the real.[23] Within the text, an anecdote opens a window onto context, so that the latter can substantiate and support the former. Anecdote steps outside the primary narrative so as to ges-

21. Olney, *Metaphors of the Self*, 31–32.

22. Nancy Miller, "Getting Personal: Autobiography as Cultural Criticism," in *Getting Personal* (New York: Routledge, 1991), 24.

23. Joel Fineman, "The History of the Anecdote: Fiction and Fiction," in *The New Historicism*, ed. Aram Veeser (New York: Routledge, 1989), 49–76.

ture more persuasively toward the real. By contrast, Miller's view of anecdote as fabrication allows us to appreciate the role of autobiography not as an attempt to create a reality effect, but as an effort to draw attention to the author's self-fiction. The point of making reference to myself and my own intentions is not to persuade you, my reader, of the "reality" of my argument, but rather to indicate the perspective from which I would like you to think that my narrative is being written. Needless to say, neither the discursive practices that have formed me nor the nature of my own intervention in those practices of history writing is transparently available to me. Nevertheless, I am assuming that my own interpretation of these cultural processes is relevant to an appreciation of the argument I have placed before you.

Returning one last time, then, to my own investment in writing this book, it is difficult for me to know what form of autobiographical myth may be most useful to understanding the perspective than informs my writing. Born to English parents in Buenos Aires, I spent my school years following both Argentine and British primary school curricula. My "experience" in school and elsewhere was complicated by the knowledge that I operated in two different cultural systems, systems that had different attitudes to just about every aspect of everyday life. Partway through my secondary education, I had to decide whether to study for entry into a British or an Argentine university. My choice of a British curriculum enabled me to appreciate the extent to which national identities are fabricated constructs dependent on processes of acculturation and education. Upon completing secondary education in Argentina, I traveled to Britain in order to attend the University of Edinburgh. Having always thought that part of me was "British," it was a nasty shock to discover that the Britain I had absorbed from my parents and their friends was the Britain of the 1940s—a very different place from the one I encountered in the 1960s. Instead of cricket and crumpets, I discovered sex, drugs and rock and roll! Graduate school and professional life in the United States confirmed what I had already suspected, that each national culture fabricates its own version of reality, and that strangers must accommodate themselves to the identifications required by each national myth.[24]

24. For theorizations of transnational hybridity, see Arjun Appadurai, *Modernity at Large: Cultural Dimensions of Globalization* (Minneapolis: University of Min-

I would argue that this potted self-fiction, one which I have characterized as both determined and empowered by conflicting national identities, can be used as a metaphor for my claim that all identities are constructed and that the scope of knowledge production must necessarily be limited and local. This self-fiction is clearly a heuristic device, a means of extracting from the complexity of my experiences some of the factors that I believe have a bearing upon my thesis; it is an assertion that myths of identity matter even if their validity cannot be substantiated in the "real." The few facts I have retrospectively culled from my experience are clearly chosen for their application to the purpose of this essay, which is to call into question history's voice from nowhere. If history writing is to be genuinely historical, then it must be capable of acknowledging the particular cultural agenda that informs its approach to the past.

It seems clear, however, that constructions of identity of the type essayed here can only be invested with cultural meaning if they coincide with the political interests of a significant sector of the population as a whole. The performance of identity can only acquire political power if it can be shared. While this might appear to disqualify my own autobiographical myth on the grounds of eccentricity, I believe that its metaphorical value may have broad appeal. The circumstances of contemporary culture are such that it is increasingly difficult to subscribe to constructions of national identity based on cultural homogeneity. The massive population movements brought about by global capitalism in the nineteenth and twentieth centuries—movements responsible, for example, for my own family's relocation from London to Buenos Aires—mean that intercultural communication as well as intercultural friction are a feature of many contemporary lives. My experience of American life, with its plethora of immigrant cultures, may have exacerbated my awareness of the limitations of my own formation. The replacement of the notion of the "melting pot" with that of the "culture wars" as the dominant trope of intercultural interaction has affected not only my own self-awareness but that of many

---

nesota Press, 1996); May Joseph, *Nomadic Identities: The Performance of Citizenship* (Minneapolis: University of Minnesota Press, 1999); and May Joseph and Jennifer Fink, eds., *Performing Hybridity* (Minneapolis: University of Minnesota Press, 1999).

other segments of the population as well. In the United States, these developments have placed a new emphasis on cultural difference, one that challenges the universalist ideology associated with the eighteenth-century rhetoric of human nature that inspired the framers of the Constitution. A bicultural background of the kind I have been describing is clearly far from exceptional. Whether the metaphorical potential inherent in this kind of experience can ever be exploited in the interests of politics dedicated to the premise that truth is a function of persuasion remains to be seen.

Contemporary theories of subjectivity thus offer the historian a paradox. They suggest that personal experience, in the form of autobiography, both matters and does not matter to an understanding of a historical text. On the one hand, autobiography can never afford us access to the relation between the historian and the text because it depends upon the fabrication of a self-fiction based on the deferred action of memory. Psychological and ideological forces also intervene to ensure that the text is forever opaque to its author. On the other hand, autobiography, or self-fiction, offers us insight into the type of self-awareness that informs the agency of a particular subjectivity. It affords the historiographer and the philosopher of history a means of comprehending some of the multitude of cultural practices that inform the writing. If autobiography does not make them available, then at least it suggests the complexity of the processes involved in the writing of history. More important, autobiographic self-fictions can serve as a form of persuasion. In articulating the particular perspective from which a tale is told, they can invite identification of those whose self-fictions coincide with that of the author, as well as those who can empathize with the nature of the subject-position in question. By giving authorial voice a location and a face, self-fictions can serve a powerful role in persuading an audience of a particular political agenda.

In conclusion, the demise of a notion of a wholly rational, autonomous subject led to the proliferation of new voices based on assertions of specific identities which had previously been repressed or occluded by the dominant paradigm. In these circumstances it has become necessary to theorize a new concept of subjectivity, one whose status as process ensures that it cannot be given stable definition. The idea of subjectivity has been rethought in terms that would have made it unrecognizable to its late lamented ancestor. In this new guise, reference to identity as agency also invokes its status as the product of those unconscious and ideological forces that haunt the production of meaning. Given this view, the writing of history can never be an entirely rational process since its narratives are always colored by the perspective of the author in question. As we have seen, the absence of an essentialist definition of identity does not necessarily exclude the possibility of informing a text with the character of a particular subject position. The paradox of autobiographic self-fictions is that they can serve as a means of creating effective narratives of persuasion.

Index